BRIGHAM'S BOYS

Enjoy the stories of
these great men,

Marlene Sullivan

BRIGHAM'S BOYS

By
Marlene Bateman Sullivan

CFI
Springville, Utah

ISBN 13: 978-1-59955-124-1

Published by CFI, an imprint of Cedar Fort, Inc., 2373 W. 700 S., Springville, UT 84663
Distributed by Cedar Fort, Inc., www.cedarfort.com

LIBRARY OF CONGRESS CATALOGING-IN-PUBLICATION DATA
Library of Congress Cataloging-in-Publication Data

Sullivan, Marlene Bateman.
Brigham's boys / Marlene Bateman Sullivan.
p. cm.
Summary: The personal story behind the men Brigham Young relied upon to
help tame the West and build up the Great Basin, focusing on the
relationship they had with Brigham and showing how they worked together to
build Zion.
ISBN 978-1-59955-124-1
1. Church of Jesus Christ of Latter-day Saints—Biography. 2.
Mormons—Biography. I. Title.

BX8693.S84 2009
289.3092'2--dc22
[B]

2008048112

Cover design by Jen Boss
Cover design © 2009 by Lyle Mortimer
Edited and typeset by Natalie A. Hepworth

Printed in the United States of America

10 9 8 7 6 5 4 3 2 1

Printed on acid-free paper

To Tana Sullivan

Contents

Preface

Brigham's Boys examines the personal story behind the men Brigham Young relied upon to help tame the West and build up the Great Basin, by focusing on the relationship they had with Brigham and showing how they worked together to build Zion. Every one of "Brigham's boys" were wholly dedicated to the kingdom of God and made incredible sacrifices, which to them were not counted as such because of their unwavering faith in God and their unswerving loyalty to Brigham Young.

In the vernacular of the day, President Young often referred to the men he worked with as his "boys." It was an affectionate term of trust and friendship. Joseph Smith also used this term occasionally. In 1834, Joseph was walking with Brigham Young and Brigham's brother, Joseph Young, when the Prophet said it was time to set up the offices of Apostles and Seventies. Joseph then said, "Brethren, I am going to call out Twelve Apostles. I think we will get together, by-and-by, and select Twelve Apostles, and select a Quorum of Seventies from those who have been up to Zion, [Zion's Camp] out of the camp boys."[1]

One of Brigham's daughters, Susa Young Gates, recalls that her father often used the term "boys." Observing how Brigham always encouraged, rather than ordered, others to follow him, Susa commented that her father would always say: " 'Come, boys,' never 'go, boys.' "[2]

Once in Salt Lake City, Brigham Young was speaking about salvation when he commented about the Saints returning to their heavenly home: "If we can pass Joseph and have him say, 'Here; you have been faithful, good boys; I hold the keys of this dispensation; I will let you pass;' then we shall be very glad."[3]

A few years after arriving in the Salt Lake Valley, Brigham mentioned the Mormon Battalion during general conference, saying, "Many of the Battalion boys are here to-day, who walked over the plains and deserts; they know what they have endured. They left their fathers, mothers, and children on the prairie."[4]

When speaking to the Territorial Legislature on 5 February 1852, Brigham said that it was his desire that God should manage governmental affairs and that the people should follow. He went on to say, "I want the Lord to rule, and be our Governor and dictate, and we are the boys to execute."[5]

Johnston's Army was advancing on Utah when Brigham Young addressed the Saints. A number of men from the Peace Commission, who were trying to negotiate a settlement, were in the audience. Brigham fearlessly stated, "We have the God of Israel—the God of battles—on our side; and, let me tell you, gentlemen, we fear not your armies. I can take a few of the boys here and, with the help of the Lord, can whip the whole of the United States. These, my brethren, put their trust in the God of Israel, and have no fears. We have proven him and he is our friend. Boys, how do you feel?"[6]

As negotiations to end the Utah War continued, Brigham was told of the dire consequences that would result if he did not allow Johnston's Army to march through Salt Lake City. After thinking the matter through, Brigham thoughtfully declared, "Well, boys, we will have to let them come in—it is for the best."[7]

As a man with sound organizational skills, Brigham Young gathered capable men to work alongside him and carry out his inspired instructions. Once the Saints had crossed the plains and reached the Salt Lake Valley, Brigham Young and his boys had the tremendous responsibility of building up Zion—a place where the Saints could flourish and be protected from persecution. The loyalty, determination, cooperation, and hard work that Brigham's boys provided were a key factors in the successful development of the Great Basin.

Brigham Young's role was to plan, protect, organize, and arrange. He left it to his boys to follow his directives and carry out his visions and goals. Some of the many responsibilities he assigned his followers were to colonize new settlements, develop agricultural and mineral production, and teach the people the gospel.

Feeling a keen responsibility toward missionary work, Brigham remarked once during conference that, "It was observed here this afternoon that it [the Spirit of the Lord] requires our boys to go into the world to preach the truth, to know that 'Mormonism' is true."[8]

Brigham called on many great men to undertake important tasks or complete special assignments. Hosea Stout was a man of great leadership abilities and as Captain of Police in Nauvoo, Winter Quarters, and Salt Lake City. Brigham relied heavily on Hosea to keep order among the Saints. Hosea was one of the first lawyers appointed to the territory and gained considerable fame as a state prosecutor and as an attorney for the United States government.

Brigham Young turned to Jesse C. Little when he needed a diplomat who could successfully negotiate with the United States Government. Brigham sent Jesse to Washington to petition for government assistance when the Saints began leaving Nauvoo. As president of the Eastern States Mission and the voice of the Church in Washington, Jesse played a vital role in the recruitment of the Mormon Battalion, which funneled desperately needed funds into the Church.

Dr. John Bernhisel was another able politician. Brigham assigned Dr. Bernhisel to go to Washington and try to promote understanding of the Mormon people. Dr. Bernhisel served as Utah's delegate to Congress in the 1850s and petitioned Congress for a territorial government.

Ephraim Hanks, Orrin Porter Rockwell, and Lot Smith were among those Brigham asked to protect himself and other leaders of the Church as they traveled to and from settlements. These men were all skilled frontiersmen whom Brigham relied on for their exceptional scouting and tracking abilities. During the Utah War, Brigham turned to Ephraim, Porter, and Lot to delay the advance of Johnston's Army in order to allow time for a mediator, Thomas L. Kane, to meet with General Johnston and other officials and negotiate a peaceful settlement.

In colonizing the west, Brigham needed leaders who would treat the

Indians fairly and honestly. One man Brigham could always rely on was Jacob Hamblin, who, with his unfailing integrity and fair treatment, won the respect and loyalty of the Indians. Jacob was renowned for his success as a peacemaker, and Brigham Young recognized his special abilities by ordaining him an Apostle to the Lamanites.

Brigham also depended on Lot Smith, another intrepid missionary to the Indians, who helped colonize Arizona. Ephraim Hanks was a courageous frontiersman, Indian agent, and pioneer who played an integral part in the settlement of the Great Basin.

Orrin Porter Rockwell also served as a missionary to the Indians and was successful in bringing about peace because the Indians respected and trusted him.

George Washington Bean was only eighteen years old when Brigham began asking him to go to the Indians and help keep the peace. George worked frequently as one of Brigham's interpreters and spent his entire lifetime promoting peace and understanding between settlers and the Indians.

Daniel W. Jones was another effective Indian missionary. As a celebrated scout, Indian interpreter, and tireless settler, Daniel was Brigham's chief mediator with a number of Indian tribes. Daniel was also one of the first missionaries to go to Mexico.

Howard Egan's reputation for honesty and dependability, along with his respect for the rights of the Indians, won him prestige and loyalty seldom seen among the natives. Howard was a hardy outdoorsman and scout who blazed trails from Utah to California and rode for the Pony Express.

The stalwart Isaac Morley was one man Brigham turned to in his colonization efforts. Because of Isaac's unique leadership capabilities, Brigham called Isaac to be a missionary to the Indians and to start a new settlement at Manti, Utah. Even though Isaac was sixty-four years old at the time, he founded a successful colony and taught many Indians the gospel.

John D. Lee was another man whom Brigham called upon to settle new areas and help build up new colonies. He helped convert a raw wilderness into profitable farms, developed large herds of livestock, and helped found settlements and erect saw, grist, and sugar-cane mills. He was an explorer and set up and operated a ferry across the Colorado River.

Thomas Ricks was another intrepid colonizer who Brigham Young relied upon. Thomas explored southern Utah and in 1859, began the new settlement of Logan, in northern Utah. Although he gained great wealth as a railroad entrepreneur, he spent all of it helping develop the Snake River country and assisting the poor. Thomas established an academy at Rexburg, Idaho, which was named Ricks Academy in his honor (though it's name was later changed to Brigham Young University-Idaho).[9]

Another man Brigham Young relied upon was Edward Hunter. Called to be the Presiding Bishop, Edward effectively supervised local bishops throughout the Church, directed the welfare program, and was the chief overseer of the Perpetual Emigrating Fund.

James S. Brown was an intrepid missionary, and Brigham knew he could count on him to go where he was directed, whether on a mission to far away islands or to explore desert regions and colonize new settlements in the west. James was often asked to speak to the Saints, and because of his uncommon, exciting, and faith-promoting experiences was able to inspire many others to serve the Lord.

Thomas Rhoades was a man with a most unusual mission. Brigham trusted him like no other when he assigned Thomas to go into the mountains and, by a special arrangement with Chief Joseph Walker and the Ute Indians, bring out gold from a secret mine and help the Church financially.

This list of men is not inclusive. There are many others Brigham trusted and relied upon, such as his brother Joseph, who worked tirelessly for the Church, and many of Brigham's own sons, notably Brigham Young Jr., who served faithfully and well. In addition, there were thousands of faithful rank-and-file Saints that demonstrated great faith and loyalty by conscientiously following Brigham's directives.

Although Brigham Young was undoubtedly one of the greatest western colonizers this country has ever seen, part of his success was due to the courage, dedication, and faith his boys demonstrated in working with the Indians, spreading the gospel to others, protecting the Saints, and creating thriving settlements in a desert wilderness. As we learn more about the men who worked alongside Brigham, and whose lives were tied so closely to his, a greater understanding will be gained of this man, who was such an outstanding leader.

Brigham's Boys focuses on the men Brigham Young relied on to carry out his vision for the Saints and gives real accounts of them, told in a frank and honest manner that makes no attempt to sanitize history. Recent polls indicate that Latter-day Saints would like historical accounts to give the full story.[10]

Despite their incredible accomplishments, the men that worked so closely with Brigham Young were still human. Although the men Brigham chose to work with had human weaknesses, they proved themselves to be uncommonly valiant servants of God.

Despite extraordinary hardships, Brigham's boys continually aligned themselves on the side of God. Their devotion to The Church of Jesus Christ of Latter-day Saints cannot be questioned. Their exceptional devotion in giving up everything they had to build up the Kingdom of God and to conscientiously fulfill every assignment Brigham gave them is awe-inspiring.

These great pioneers had a bright hope for the future. All of us today are blessed by their matchless legacy of faith and sacrifice.

Notes

1. *Journal of Discourses*, vol. 9, 7 May 1861, 26 volumes (London: 1854–86), 89.

2. Susa Young Gates in collaboration with Leah D. Widtstoe, *The Life Story of Brigham Young* (New York: The Macmillan Company, 1930), 212.

3. *Journal of Discourses*, vol. 5, 7 October 1857, 26 volumes (London: 1854–86), 332.

4. *Journal of Discourses*, vol. 2, 18 February 1855, 26 volumes (London: 1854–86), 186.

5. Fred C. Collier, comp., *The Teachings of Brigham Young, 1852–1854*, vol. 3, (Salt Lake City: Collier's Publishing, 1987), 46.

6. Edward W. Tullidge, *Life of Brigham Young or Utah and Her Founders*, 313.

7. William Hickman and John Hanson Beadle, *Brigham's Destroying Angel: Being the Life, Confession, and Startling Disclosures of the Notorious Bill Hickman, the Danite Chief of Utah* (Salt Lake City: Shepard Publishing Company, 1904), 130.

8. *Journal of Discourses*, vol. 11, 29 April 1866, 26 volumes (London: 1854–86), 215.

9. Steven D. Bennion, "Thomas E. Ricks," *Pioneer*, Autumn 2001, 17.

10. *The Salt Lake Tribune*, 21 July, 2007, C3.

George Washington Bean

1831–1897

Having been warned that the Indians might be planning to attack, George Washington Bean and Orrin Porter Rockwell approached the Indian village cautiously. Instead of riding in like they would normally have done, they dismounted nearby and hid behind some thick brush to see what was going on in the village. The rumors of war were confirmed when they saw the Indians making preparations for war.

The year was 1849, and Brigham Young had sent George and Porter to deliver a message of peace and friendship to the Indians. But realizing the danger they were in, George and Porter each said to the other, "If we both go on horseback, we'll be killed."[1] Still, they were determined to do what Brigham Young had asked.

George declared, "We were humble, yet fearless, because the Prophet of the Lord had called us to service. We accepted it. We knew the Indians were in their war-paint, holding war dances about their campfires. Since some Indians had killed cows and stolen horses, we moved cautiously and prayerfully. I never carried a gun on any Indian mission but Porter always was well armed since the days of the mobbing of Nauvoo."[2]

George and Porter decided that George should go in alone. Porter would stay hidden, waiting for a sign from George and ready to rush in if help was needed.

George relates what happened next:

> Brother Brigham [had] sent us with a message of Peace, and a "God Bless You," so I went forward without fear. As I neared the camp, I saw them dancing about a bonfire, with their paints and feathers, and squaws beating tom-toms. When they saw a man coming, they feared, and three "bucks" came out to meet me, tied my hands behind me . . . and stood me on a buffalo robe and there I stood for two hours.
>
> I was not permitted to say a word until after they had related all their bad feelings; boasted over their depredations and successful battles with other tribes, too numerous to mention; and told what they expected to do with the "Whites" now stealing their hunting grounds and how the crows would pick our bones, etc.
>
> Being over six feet tall, much taller than any of them, and stretching up still taller as they talked, calm and fearless, there I stood for two long hours. When they saw I was not afraid but friendly, one war-horse Indian after another slunk away . . . The "Gift of Interpretation" was given to me, as I called it, for I understood every word they said.
>
> Finally, the Indians allowed [me] to speak. I delivered the message of friendship from the "White Chief" Brigham Young, who represented the "Great Spirit" in his feelings toward the Indians and all mankind, a brotherly feeling that must last forever, etc. The dancers stopped and listened.[3]

When George told the Indians that his companion was waiting outside the village, they allowed him to go get Porter and bring him into camp. Porter then delivered a similar message to them from Brigham Young. The Indians decided the two men were true messengers and gave them a promise of peace. George said, "Many of those Indians became friendly and became protectors of my life, and warned the people, through me, of dangers. I was eighteen years old at this time, but grown up through hard experiences."[4]

After this harrowing experience, George and Porter rode to Salt Lake City and told President Young about their visit. President Young was very pleased that they had successfully averted war. He asked the two men to continue taking the message to all Indian tribes and let them know that the Saints were there to build homes, raise cattle and grain, and teach them. Brigham ended by saying, "Now, George and Porter, be true to yourselves and your mission and when you feel prompted to visit an Indian individual or Camp, pray for guidance in both speech and action, that good may come from that visit. God bless you."[5]

Although George was still a teenager, he appeared much older than his years and was eminently suited to serve as a missionary to the Indians. George Washington Bean was born in Mendon, Illinois, on 1 April 1831 and was baptized when he was ten years old. George was big for his age and was just barely into his teens when he joined a posse led by Jacob B. Backenstos, the Sheriff of Hancock Country, whose job was to stop the mobs from burning homes and destroying crops. He was ordained a Seventy when he was fourteen years old and guarded the temple in Nauvoo temple at night.[6]

When the Saints left Nauvoo, George went with his married sister, Sarah Ann, and her baby and assisted her in crossing the plains in 1847, while the rest of his family stayed behind. George said, "Thus was I, a lad of sixteen, launched forth on a journey of one thousand miles in charge of a team of four oxen and a family."[7]

When his company neared the Sweetwater River, George met President Brigham Young, who had been to the Salt Lake Valley and was now returning to Winter Quarters.

The following year, in May 1848, Brigham issued a call for men and teams to go back East to help more Saints move to Utah. George volunteered, and on this trip, was able to help his parents and siblings cross the plains.

In 1849, Brigham asked George and a group of thirty men to settle in Utah Valley, to farm, fish, and teach the Indians about farming. As his group was nearing the site where they hoped to settle, they were met by a young brave, Angatewats, who forbade them from going any further.[8] One of the men asked Angatewats to give them a chance, saying that if the Indians would let them settle there, they would prove that they could live in peace. Angatewats went to discuss their petition with his tribe, who then decided to let the Mormons settle on their land.

Living close to the Indians allowed George to learn their language and more about their culture. He said, "During this Summer of 1849, being interested in the Indians, I soon made friends, [and] learned much of their language and gesticulations."[9]

Then, George suffered a terrible injury. He was helping William Dayton fire a cannon, when it exploded. William was killed instantly and

George was thrown thirty feet by the explosion. His left hand was found on the ground by a nearby house. Although he was still breathing, George was so mangled and lacerated that no one thought he would live. They sent for a doctor who amputated George's lower left arm, leaving a three and a half-inch stump which George said, "Served me well all my life. Of course in those days people had to endure pain in operations by the will power of the injured."[10]

The doctor treated his burns and extracted as many of the large splinters that were embedded in his body as he could, but was unable to get them all out. George said, "Two hundred splinters remained in my body for twenty years, working to the surface at different times."[11]

George's entire face scabbed over, leaving him blind. Three weeks after the accident, President Brigham Young, Heber C. Kimball and Willard Richards came to see him. George said:

> Why did these three men, the Presidency of the Church of Jesus Christ in these latter days, come to see and bless an insignificant eighteen year old boy like me? . . . I could not see them, but recognized their voices . . . Mother appealed to them—"Brother Brigham, do you think he can live?"
>
> "Of course he can, and will," he answered. Then he came to me, took my hand, the right hand, the only one I had—and asked: "George, do you want to live?"
>
> "Yes, if I can do any good."
>
> President Young then said: "Then you shall live."[12]

Brigham called his counselors to gather around the bed, and together they anointed George and gave him a blessing. George said that when President Young "rebuked the power of the Destroyer from my body. . . . It was like an electric current that ran through me from head to foot and it took the severe pain with it. He [Brigham] pled with the Lord to heal me from head to foot that all wounds might heal quickly. . . . He made plain to me that the Holy Ghost, bestowed upon me after baptism, would be my constant guide and educator and that the Lord's work assigned to me will be gloriously completed." George said, "My life of despair was changed by the visit of these three Prophets of the Lord. . . . Next day the scales fell from my eyes and I saw the glorious light."[13]

Being able to see again gave George hope for the future. During his long and difficult convalescence, Chief Sanpitch and other Indians came to visit, and George spent his time learning their language better. He also began studying Shoshone and Spanish.

When he was somewhat recovered, George began teaching school. In the spring of 1851, he was elected city recorder for the city of Provo. That same year, Brigham Young asked George to accompany him on a four-week trip to Southern Utah. On the way south, their company met a group of people traveling near the Sevier River. President Young felt it was too dangerous for the emigrants to cross the Sevier River alone, so asked George and three other men to help them across.

Later that spring, when a territorial form of government had been established, George Washington Bean was appointed as a deputy marshal to Joseph L. Haywood, a United States Marshal. Brigham often asked George to travel with him as his interpreter when President Young would go meet with Mexican traders in an attempt to stop them from buying and selling children.

George married Elizabeth Baum on 6 January 1853, when he was twenty-two years old. In later years, he practiced polygamy.

The Walker War occurred during 1853 and 1854. This costly war between the whites and Ute Indians resulted in the deaths of thirty settlers and widespread destruction of buildings, crops, and livestock. During this time, George was heavily involved in peace negotiations, working directly with Brigham Young.

George said, "My time was spent in guard service and in moving about among all the Indians that could be reached and using my influence to keep them from joining the hostiles. In this line of service I traveled to all parts of the Territory and no doubt much good was accomplished, as we often had messages from President Young to take to the leading Chiefs and I could speak their language when we visited."[14]

He met with many different Indian tribes in an effort to promote peace. George said, "I was also to see the Indians on Green River and Sandys. I had many stormy debates with them and some hairbreadth escapes from their savage fury, but the Lord was my guide and protector."[15]

One winter, George was assigned, along with a small group of men, to visit a distant Indian village. It was rigorous work breaking trail for the pack animals while crossing the Uintah Mountains, and they could only go five miles a day. At night, the men slept in snow that was up to twenty-feet deep.

While living and working among the Indians, George made many friends but Washear was one of his truest friends. Washear visited George frequently while he was recovering from his accident and helped George learn the Indian language. Many times, Washear was able to warn George of danger, and in 1853, he saved George's life.

This incident occurred one day when Washear was visiting with George and his wife, Elizabeth. A Ute Indian doctor stopped by to tell George that his wife (the Indian doctor's) and child had just died. The doctor explained that he wanted some good person to go with them to the next life. (It was a custom among the Indians for them to kill other people and animals to "accompany" the departed person to heaven.)

As the doctor stepped closer to George, commenting that he was a very good person, Elizabeth saw the point of a hunting knife extending from a blanket the doctor was holding. She quickly shouted a warning. As she did, the doctor raised his arm to plunge the knife into George.

In a flash, Washear threw his bow and arrows at the doctor, deflecting the knife. He then began wrestling with the doctor, who managed to break free and run away.

The next day, the doctor came back. He asked George to forgive him, explaining that he had been so crazed by the death of his wife and child that he had tried to kill the best friend the Indians had ever had. George commented afterwards that this incident made the missionaries realize they had work to do in trying to put an end to the Ute custom of killing others to accompany the dead to the next life.

A crisis between the Indians and the settlers occurred in October of 1854, when Chief Walker went to Nephi and found the Mormons building a fort. He was very insulted, feeling that building a fort was proof the settlers wanted to keep the Indians away. Chief Walker angrily reminded the Saints that he had given Brigham and his people the privilege of settling on his land, but if they continued to separate themselves and fence off their settlements and build forts to stay inside, away from his people, the Indians would not allow the whites to continue getting wood or grass on the outside.

Work was halted on the fort and an urgent message was sent to Brigham Young. President Young wrote a strongly-worded letter and asked George Bean and Porter Rockwell to deliver it to Chief Walker. He also had them take supplies so they could trade with the Indians. In his letter, Brigham told Chief Walker that he was foolish to oppose the building of walls around the settlements and warned him that the Mormons were doing the Lord's work and that Chief Walker and his people ought to mind their own business and the Saints would do the same.

When George finished reading the message, Chief Walker crossly snatched the letter from his hand, threw it on the ground, and after trampling it under his feet, said he was going to declare war.

George said, "I picked up the letter of President Young's from under Walker's feet and told him I would return to Salt Lake and tell Brigham how his words of counsel had been treated by him."

Chief Walker flew into a rage and said, "No, you won't go and get all the Mormons after us again."

Changing direction, Chief Walker then asked George what he was going to do with all the supplies that he had brought from Salt Lake City. George replied that he would take them back. Chief Walker said he would not allow that, as he wanted them.

At that point, Washear spoke up and told the chief: "Brigham . . . wants you to do right and not act foolish . . . [George] is only talking for Brigham, and he wants you to listen and do right and all will be well."[16]

After discussing the matter further, George, Porter, and Washear were allowed to leave and go to Nephi, a nearby settlement. Not long after, Chief Walker arrived in Nephi with his little son. He told George, "I'm not angry now. 'Shenentz', my relative, has convinced me I was wrong in my suspicions of Brigham and his Mormons and I'm sorry for all the trouble." He then asked George if they could trade goods.

The trading went on for five days. Although there were several more stormy arguments, and the Mormons had to take eight Indian slaves to prevent them from being killed by the Utes, peace prevailed in the end. George said, "These hair-raising experiences gave evidence that the Lord can raise up a protective power from a source the least expected when it becomes necessary."[17]

George faced yet another life-and-death situation in August of 1854 or 1855. It all began when Shoshone Indians attacked a group of Utes, killing four and wounding two. When the Shoshones went to President Isaac Higbee's home, Isaac sent for George to come and interpret for him. Shortly after the Shoshone Indians left, a group of Ute Indians, painted black and red and ready for war, came to President Higbee's house.

The Utes asked for guns and ammunition so they could fight the Shoshones. When they discovered that George had acted as an interpreter for the Shoshones, they were furious, feeling this was proof George was friendly with their enemies, the Shoshones.

A fight broke out as the Utes attacked him. George said that the Indians would have killed him except that "old Chief Pe-teet-neet rushed to me on his horse, bent over me and shielded me, all the time pleading for my life. . . . The Indians gave me up for the present, warning me they would settle at another time."[18]

The Utes didn't linger as they were in a hurry to catch up with the Shoshones. After battling the Shoshones, the Utes returned. Believing that the Mormons, especially George, had sent for the Shoshones and asked them to kill the Utes, they ordered the Mormons off their land. Explanations did no good and for two weeks, Ute scouts returned daily to threaten George.

One time, George was away from the settlement when he noticed a cloud of dust caused by a galloping band of Ute Indians. He wheeled around and raced back to the settlement. Seeing a barn, George dismounted and ran inside to hide, telling the startled men not to say anything about him to the Indians. When the Utes arrived, they searched the barn thoroughly but could not find George, even though they came within a few feet of where he was hiding.[19]

In 1855, George heard a rumor that he had been called to the Las Vegas Indian Mission. Since he had recently been offered several jobs as an interpreter at good pay, he went to see President Young to find out if the rumors were true. They were. Brigham told George he wanted him to work among the Piede Indians and interpret for a group of people who had been called to start a new settlement in Las Vegas.

President Young then asked George how he liked being called as a missionary. George replied, "I told him that I loved my religion above all else and that I was ready to go where ever I could serve the Kingdom best. He was pleased with the answer and blessed me."[20]

Shortly before he left on this assignment, a group of soldiers, led by Lieutenant Sylvester Mowry, asked George to accompany them partway to California by way of Las Vegas. George accepted and was able to earn three dollars a day by acting as an interpreter and guide while traveling to his mission.[21]

When the missionaries arrived in Las Vegas, they immediately began to clear the land and plant crops. The local Indians were shy at first, but the missionaries soon won them over by being friendly and treating them with respect and kindness. The Indians began to help cultivate the ground while George learned their language. "As interpreter, George W. Bean had a central role in the missionary band of thirty-three men who took up their labors in the desert . . . he had to learn a second difficult Shoshonean language."[22]

Although the missionaries and Indians suffered terribly from the heat while cultivating the land, there was a good crop the first year. The Indians continued to work alongside the missionaries, helping to clear more land, make adobes, and herd the stock. A few Indians accepted the gospel and were converted. Besides working as an interpreter and helping tend crops, George and a few other men did some exploring. He said, "The purpose of our explorations was to extend acquaintance with all the Indian Tribes and Bands." During their travels, the missionaries became acquainted with the Pahgahts, the Pahruchats, the Panominch, the Quoeech, and the Mohaves.[23] While on this mission, George was asked to take a census of natives within the mission boundaries. Since the mission boundaries were so vast, George and his companions had to travel almost constantly.

George relates one interesting experience: "We were cornered on this trip by Chief Thomas' hostile Indians who required us to heal a very sick girl forthwith or we could go no farther. We were five in number, and if Elders were ever united in Faith and administration to the sick it was us at that time, for we saw that the Natives were well prepared to carry out their threats. The Lord was with us, however, and He preserved the little girl's life, and I may say ours, until we got peacefully and safely away from them."[24]

George went home briefly in March of 1856 to report on the mission, help at home on his farm, and to request that more settlers be sent to the area. He returned to Las Vegas in June and continued his missionary labors. After lead was discovered nearby, some of the missionaries began mining. In September, George and Thomas E. Ricks were asked to take a load of lead to Salt Lake City.

George said, "A ton of lead ore was shipped with each of us, which was sold to Salt Lake potters. He [Thomas Ricks] and I were both cripples, one armed men, yet we struggled through the 500 miles, each driving four mule teams. . . . My children never could imagine how we harnessed the mules, put on the brake and handled four lines in going into a hollow and releasing the brakes when ascending—all with just one hand. It was a problem for many years to learn how to make one hand do for two."[25]

In 1857, Brigham Young found out that President Buchanan was sending troops to Utah. He asked George to notify people in the outlying settlements in Nevada to sell out and return to Utah. George writes: "My part was to go to Carson Valley in Nevada in company with Peter W. Conover as captain and O. P. Huntington as guide. We were to take a direct course across the deserts and make the trip as quickly as possible . . . our guide became mystified, got off the track, and we spent eighteen days on the trip, got out of provisions, lived on poor horse meat for three days, and suffered much from lack of water."[26]

In March of 1858, Brigham asked George to take a group of men and explore the desert west of Fillmore and Beaver. Their assignment was to find hiding places for the Saints in case Johnston's Army invaded Utah. George and his men were exploring the area around Beaver when a terrible snowstorm hit. It snowed continually for twenty-seven hours. With the wind blowing a gale, the men dug holes in the ground to try and save themselves. When the storm finally ended, five horses were dead, the wagon covers were ripped to shreds, and their cattle was scattered.[27]

In February of 1865, Major Kinney, an Indian Agent, was notified that Ute Indians were starving in Sanpete Valley. Major Kinney and George Bean organized a relief party and took provisions to the Indians.

A few months later, the Black Hawk War broke out. George was kept busy carrying messages back and forth between the whites and the settlers. General Morrow asked George to set up a peace conference with the Indians, but they refused to meet. George spent several days trying to persuade them and in the end, they agreed to meet with the general. George said that the Indians would never have met with the General had he not been there. George said of the Indians, "We were true friends, and I spoke their language, and we understood each other in word and spirit."[28]

After the Indians went over their grievances with General Morrow, they asked to go to Washington and explain their position to President Ulysses S. Grant. When General Morrow agreed to this, George went to Salt Lake City and talked with Brigham Young, who felt that much good could come from such a visit.

George Washington Bean went as an interpreter, accompanying four Indian Chiefs and Mr. Dodge, an Indian Agent. The men left Salt Lake City by train on 17 October 1872. During the trip, George said he was about worn out answering the Indian's many questions . . . He later said, "The President [Grant] received us kindly and enjoyed meeting the Natives. He seemed to know our needs which made it a very profitable trip for all concerned."[29]

George Washington Bean died in Richfield, Utah, on 9 December 1897. He was adventurous, courageous, and resourceful, always using his talents to promote peace and to preach the gospel. An extraordinary pioneer who served a frontiersman's role in exploring new country, George worked among the Indians as an interpreter, peacemaker, and missionary. He was also an important leader in civic affairs. He held many offices, including Territorial Indian Interpreter, Deputy United States Marshal, Lieutenant Colonel of the Nauvoo Legion, assessor and collector in Utah County, assistant collector of Internal Revenue; member of the Territorial Legislature, probate judge in Utah country (1874), and prosecuting attorney of Utah County. After his move to Sevier County in 1873, George served as Probate Judge of Sevier County.[30]

Notes

1.   Flora Diana Bean Horne, comp., *Autobiography of George Washington Bean, A Utah Pioneer of 1847 and His Family Records* (Salt Lake City: Utah Printing, 1945), 53.

2.   Ibid.

3.   Ibid.

4.   Ibid., 54.

5.   Ibid., 55.

6.   Ibid., 21–23.

7.   Ibid., 32

8.   Ibid., 50.

9.   Ibid., 52.

10. Ibid., 58–59.

11. Ibid., 60.

12. Ibid., 60–61.

13. Ibid.

14. Ibid., 92.

15. Ibid., 95.

16. Ibid., 99.

17. Ibid., 100.

18. Ibid., 107.

19. Ibid., 108–9.

20. Ibid., 115.

21. Clyde A. Milner II and Floyd A. O'Neil, eds., *Churchmen and the Western Indians, 1820–1920* (Norman: University of Oklahoma Press), 91.

22. Ibid.

23. Horne, comp., *Autobiography of George Washington Bean, A Utah Pioneer of 1847 and His Family Records*, 120.

24. Ibid., 122–23.

25. Ibid., 124–25.

26. Merrill D. Beal, *Henry Allen Beal and George Washington Bean, Pioneers on the Utah Frontier* (Garland: V. W. Johns, Printing, 1971), 129.

27. Ibid., 130.

28. Horne, comp., *Autobiography of George Washington Bean, A Utah Pioneer of 1847 and His Family Records*, 162–163.

29. Ibid., 164.

30. Beal, *Henry Allen Beal and George Washington Bean, Pioneers on the Utah Frontier*, 130.

John M. Bernhisel

1799–1881

The Saints had only been in Utah a short time when Brigham Young asked Dr. John M. Bernhisel to go to Washington, DC and serve as a liaison between The Church of Jesus Christ of Latter-day Saints and the federal government. This assignment was a tough one, especially since federal officials sometimes found Brigham lacking in diplomacy and his personality too forthright for their liking. Since Brigham could be brutally frank at times and had never been one to bridle his tongue, this had a dampening effect on Dr. Bernhisel's efforts to develop good relations between Utah and the federal government.

As Utah's first delegate to Congress, Dr. Bernhisel had his hands full in Washington as he tried to smooth the ruffled feelings of the public, politicians, and presidents who had been angered by the outspoken leader of the Church. Part of the problem was that Brigham's speeches, written for the Saints, were often taken out of context and used as fodder for Eastern newspapers, which were only too happy to print Brigham's most inflammatory statements. It didn't help that Brigham was distrustful and often openly scornful of the same government that Dr. Bernhisel worked with on a daily basis. Time and again, John's role was to try to clear up misunderstandings over Brigham's fiery rhetoric which the public and politicians found so infuriating.

Dr. John Milton Bernhisel was born 23 June 1799, in Pennsylvania and graduated from the University of Pennsylvania in 1827 with a medical degree. John was a tall, dignified physician, who was close to Joseph Smith, and later to Brigham Young. Dr. Bernhisel served as a bishop for a time. When it was decided to bond the Twelve Apostles as they went about collecting money for the Nauvoo Temple, John volunteered to be a bondsman for Brigham, for the sum of $2,000.[1]

In March of 1844, John met with the Prophet Joseph and other leaders to discuss how the Saints could obtain their constitutional rights from the United States government. Noting John's special diplomatic abilities, Joseph Smith asked Dr. Bernhisel to write to Governor Ford regarding the losses the Saints had suffered because of persecution. As events proceeded, John testified in court that the Saints were alarmed because mobs were openly making preparations to attack Nauvoo.

After Joseph Smith was killed, John supported Brigham Young as the new Prophet of the Church. John Bernhisel married Julia Ann Van Orden in 1845, and they came west when Brigham Young led the Saints to their new home in the Salt Lake Valley.

When Brigham decided to petition Congress for Utah to become a territory, he sent Dr. Bernhisel to Washington, D.C. in January of 1849. John was an intelligent, well-respected individual and, with his political shrewdness, was an ideal person to present the petition to Congress. Brigham Young knew that John had the political astuteness that would help the Church further important causes in the vast political arena in Washington, DC. Aware that the Church had its enemies, Brigham asked his brother Lorenzo Young to act as a bodyguard for Dr. Bernhisel when he left on 3 May 1849 with the petition that bore 2,270 signatures.[2]

In Washington, Dr. Bernhisel patiently lobbied to gain territorial status for Utah, as well as the appointment of Mormons—or at least men who were friendly to the Church—to territorial offices. Glen Barrett, a professor of history at Boise State University, said John M. Bernhisel "was an indefatigable lobbyist who made a favorable impression upon congressional leaders as well as Presidents, and was instrumental in procuring appropriations for a territorial library, roads, mail, and telegraph service."[3]

When Congress proved reluctant to take action on the petition,

Dr. Bernhisel managed to get an appointment with President Millard Fillmore to discuss the matter. Besides talking about Utah receiving territorial status, John also pressed to have Brigham appointed as governor. When President Fillmore admitted that he had some concerns about Brigham's loyalty, Dr. Bernhisel assured him that Brigham was trustworthy. Afterwards, perhaps to emphasize what was expected, John wrote to Brigham, saying, "He [President Fillmore] inquired whether you would support the administration if you should be appointed. I replied that I thought you would."[4]

In September of 1850, both houses passed the bill and President Millard Fillmore signed it, creating the Territory of Utah. In addition to securing the territorial government status and boundaries he had requested, John was pleased when President Fillmore agreed to appoint Brigham Young as governor and three other Mormons to serve as territorial officers.

Dr. Bernhisel wrote Brigham about the good news: "I have labored with my pen and otherwise used my best endeavors to obtain a consummation so devoutly to be wished and I am gratified to be able to inform you that my efforts were crowned with complete success. What I wished was that the 37th parallel should form the southern and the crest of the Rocky Mountains, the eastern boundaries. These limits were established just before the bill was ordered to be engrossed."[5]

Dr. Bernhisel returned to Salt Lake City on 19 July 1851, accompanied by two newly-appointed federal justices, Broughton D. Harris and Lemuel G. Brandebury, and a federal Indian agent, Henry R. Day. They officials brought with them $20,000, which would help the people in Utah establish a new territorial government.[6]

Unfortunately, problems quickly arose when the justices found out that Brigham Young had already called for an election of legislators and had begun taking a census. Brigham felt it was necessary to move forward in a prompt and efficient manner, but the justices felt Brigham was overstepping his authority.

Harris, Brandebury, and Day felt that these procedures should only have been undertaken under their supervision. They declared that Brigham's actions were precipitous and dismissive of the law. The federal officials were not moved when Brigham explained that he had called for an election and began taking the census so that legislative and judicial districts could be established and representatives elected in time to travel to Washington before inclement weather arrived, which would prevent the representatives from leaving Utah until spring.

John did his best to smooth over this disagreement, but it was a sour beginning. Further conflicts occurred when, during a Pioneer Day (July 24) celebration, the officials became offended at a strongly-worded speech from Daniel Wells that was highly critical of the government. Addressing the Saints, Daniel related the persecution they had suffered and expressed his outrage that they had received no aid nor redress from the United States government, which had freely allowed them to be robbed and murdered. Brigham Young had a few vitriolic comments of his own to add, stating that those who had worked against the Saints (a reference to the late United States President Zachary Taylor) would die an untimely death and end up in hell. Other speeches during the day continued to heavily criticize the government.[7]

A week and a half later, the first general election for the brand-new Utah Territory was held on 4 August 1851. John M. Bernhisel had proven himself such an able politician during territorial negotiations that he was elected as Utah's first congressional delegate.

After his election to Congress, it didn't take long before the eminently capable Dr. Bernhisel became a well-known and well-respected figure in Washington. Because of his acumen, good judgment, and extensive political connections, he was able to use his influence to benefit the Church. Dr. Bernhisel was reelected three more times and served as a delegate for Utah for ten years.

At the end of August 1851, another federally appointed justice, Perry E. Brocchus, arrived in Salt Lake City. Brocchus had wanted to serve as Utah's Territorial Representative and was disappointed to learn that elections had already been held. The other federal officials, Broughton D. Harris, Lemuel G. Brandebury, and Henry R. Day, wasted no time informing Brocchus about the offensive, Pioneer Day speeches. Outraged, Brocchus asked to see the printed text of Daniel Wells' speech. After reading it, he asked for permission to address the Saints.

During a church meeting, Judge Brocchus thoroughly criticized Daniel Wells and Brigham Young for their comments about the government. Then he told the audience that the government had requested a piece of stone to be sent back east, which would be used in building the Washington Monument. However, he stated his request in such a way that the Saints were infuriated:

"I have a commission from the Washington Monument Association to ask of you a block of marble as the test of your loyalty to the government of the United States. But in order for you to do it acceptably, you must become virtuous, and teach your daughters to become virtuous, or your offering had better remain in the bosom of your native mountains."[8]

There was an immediate uproar from the audience, who were outraged at his remarks. President Young strode to the podium and after a few sharp comments, declared that the people were loyal to the government and for Brocchus to ask the Saints to become virtuous was an insult. He invited Brocchus to apologize but the justice declined. Later, Brigham said he wasn't the only angry person that night and that "the sisters alone felt indignant enough to have chopped him [Brocchus] in pieces."[9]

An exchange of letters between President Young and Brocchus did not ease hostilities. The divide continued to deepen, until—without warning—Brocchus and the other officials left the territory at the end of September, taking with them the $20,000 they had brought to establish the fledging territory. After their abrupt departure, they were often referred to as the "runaway justices."

In Washington, the justices told President Fillmore that Brigham's irregular procedures, despotism, and hostility toward the United States had made it impossible for them to function. The main complainants, Perry E. Brocchus and Broughton D. Harris declared, were that the Mormons were immoral, disloyal fanatics and were led by a despotic man. Brocchus further stated that they had been compelled to flee for their lives because of Governor Young's lawless acts.

John M. Bernhisel, Utah's representative in Washington, read the official report submitted by Brandebury, Harris, Brocchus, and Day, and quickly wrote Brigham, asking for a full explanation. In his letter, John warned Brigham that this incident could have serious repercussions, perhaps even resulting in troops being sent to Utah. Brigham wrote back, saying he felt calm about the situation and was sure that the citizens of the United States would protest and stop the President if he decided to send out troops. Brigham then added that, if need be, he was willing to move the Saints again.[10]

John then began working to stem the tide of misunderstandings arising from the Brocchus Report, as it was called. In January of 1852, Dr. Bernhisel publicly denounced the report, maintaining it contained grossly exaggerated, if not false and perverted, statements. He then asked the Speaker of the House to appoint a commission to investigate the charges.

Brigham Young sent one of his counselors, Jedediah Grant, to assist Dr. Bernhisel in Washington, but Dr. Bernhisel was wary of the quick-tempered Apostle who was known as being even more outspoken than Brigham. Afraid that Jedediah might do more damage than good, Dr. Bernhisel would not, at first, even introduce him to important political figures.

In April, President Millard Fillmore invited Dr. Bernhisel to visit him to discuss the Brocchus Report and the appointment of new territorial officers to replace those that had "run away." President Fillmore assured Dr. Bernhisel that he did not join in the current prejudice against the Mormons and that he wanted to do justice to them, while fulfilling his duty to the government. When asked if there was any truth to the report that the Mormons had set up a government for themselves, John assured the president that this was not the case.

Dr. Bernhisel continued to counter the justices' claims by writing articles for newspapers and by meeting with politicians. Finally, in July, he triumphantly wrote Brigham Young, saying that the "runaway justices" had been beaten on every point they had brought up against the people of Utah.

When President Fillmore appointed Lazarus Reid, Benjamin Ferris, and Leonidas Shaver as the new officials to the Utah Territory, Dr. Bernhisel was pleased. He told Brigham Young that although these men were not members of the Church, they were far different men than Brandebury, Harris, Brocchus, and Day. He urged Brigham to make sure these new appointees were warmly received.

Apparently, Dr. Bernhisel had some concerns that Brigham, who was known for his bluntness, might say something that would ignite more controversy. He warned Brigham against this, saying, "If there shall be another flare up we shall be utterly ruined here as regards to obtaining of appropriations or even retaining any offices in our territory." John firmly told President Young "that no pains nor effort be spared to cultivate the most friendly relation between the new appointees and the authorities and people of Utah."

Brigham wrote back, assuring the doctor that all would be well, replying jovially, "Be of good courage doctor, for all is right. Do not permit anything that may occur discourage you in the least. Go ahead never doubting although the sun and all else may appear dark around you."[11]

When Judges H. Reid and Leonidas Shaver arrived in Utah Territory,

Brigham wrote Dr. Bernhisel, saying that he was pleased with the two men, and that they "conduct themselves very gentlemanly thus far, appear frank, and friendly in their deportment and are universally liked, and respected in their Offices."[12]

After he had been in Utah for some time, Chief Justice Reid made the following comment, "I have made up my mind that no man has been more grossly misrepresented than Governor Young, and that he is a man who will reciprocate kindness and good intentions as heartily and freely as any one, but if abused, or crowded hard, I think he may be found exceedingly hard to handle."[13]

Despite his previous written reassurances to Dr. Bernhisel that he would be careful with his comments, Brigham continued to speak his mind. Dr. Bernhisel was kept busy explaining some of President Young's less temperate statements, such as when Brigham openly defied government authority by declaring he would remain in office until the Lord Almighty told him he didn't need to be governor any longer.[14]

Once, Dr. Bernhisel sent Brigham an inflammatory article that had been published in the *Baltimore Daily Sun* that contained some of Brigham Young's more confrontational statements. Once again, Dr. Bernhisel warned Brigham that his defiant pronouncements, even though intended for the Saints' ears only, could "frequently be twisted or tortured so as to rebound to your injury or the injury of the entire church." Dr. Bernhisel also said that because Brigham continued to reel off incendiary statements, he had "to meet all of these things here face to face and explain, palliate, contradict, deny, as the case may be."[15]

Brigham wrote back at length, elaborating on his belief that since God ruled over the affairs of men, it did not matter what kings or officers of state did. He then wrote directly to the *Baltimore Daily Sun* to explain himself more fully. Unfortunately, in his letter, Brigham defiantly declared once more that "President Pierce and all hell could not remove me from Office," causing further uproar.[16]

Such remarks greatly increased opposition against Brigham Young, the Mormons, and Utah in general. The public announcement in 1852 about the practice of plural marriage further exacerbated public concerns.

A year later, John Bernhisel was reelected as a congressional delegate. He immediately began lobbying to have Brigham Young, whose appointment was officially over in 1854, reappointed as governor. However, when John asked President Pierce about this, the president replied that there was too much prejudice against the Mormons for him to allow Brigham Young to continue on as governor.

Early the following year, Brigham Young told the Saints, "The newspapers are teeming with statements that I said, 'President Pierce and all hell could not remove me from office.' I will tell you what I did say . . . the Lord reigns and rules in the armies of the heavens, and does His pleasure among the inhabitants of the earth. He sets up a kingdom here, and pulls down another there. . . . He makes Kings, Presidents, and Governor at His pleasure; hence I conclude that I shall be Governor of Utah Territory, just as long as He wants me to be and for that time, neither the President of the United States, nor any other power, can prevent it."[17]

Bowing to public pressure, President Pierce appointed Colonel Edward J. Steptoe as the new governor of Utah. Steptoe, however, had been stationed in the new territory and knew how firmly the Saints were behind Brigham. Not only did he refuse to accept the appointment, he even signed a petition requesting that Brigham Young be reappointed. Unsettled by Steptoe's refusal, President Pierce decided to take no action for the time being, thus allowing Brigham Young to remain as governor.

Brigham and Dr. Bernhisel continued to correspond frequently. President Young's letters were filled with detailed questions, instructions, and requests for information, which Dr. Bernhisel answered meticulously. Although Brigham asked John to begin working toward the admission of Utah into the union as a free and independent state, it would be over forty years before this would occur.[18]

During the next few years, John continued to work as a mediator between an impatient, and sometimes brutally frank Brigham Young, and a government who always seemed ready to believe the worst of the Mormons.

Dr. Bernhisel was reelected as a delegate once again in 1855, but was disappointed when every request he made for statehood was denied. In 1856, Brigham replied calmly to one of John's melancholy letters, written when yet another request for Utah to be admitted into the union had been denied. Brigham told him not to despair. "For you know that our path sometimes leads through gloomy scenes. . . . I trust that when our application is fairly before them it will be favorably considered and acted upon. The Lord will control all for our good."[19]

After James Buchanan became president in 1857, John Bernhisel asked him to retain Brigham Young as governor. Buchanan denied the request, stating that sending Brigham's name to the Senate would raise a firestorm. John said that he quite understood President Buchanan's fears, which was why he did not ask for Brigham to be reappointed, just held over.[20]

A crisis occurred in 1857 when new allegations and charges of wrong doing were made against Brigham Young. Another disgruntled justice, W. W. Drummond, accused Brigham of destroying government papers. He also told President Buchanan that the Mormons were disloyal and rebellious. Without investigating the charges, President James Buchanan acted precipitously, mobilizing an army of 2,500 soldiers and auxiliaries under General Albert Johnston and sending them to establish law and order. He also appointed a new governor, Alfred Cumming, and other officials who traveled with Johnston's army.

Buchanan's hasty decision seems to be based mainly on the nation's heavy disapproval of the Mormons, which reached high levels because of Brigham's outspokenness, the scandal associated with the "runaway justices," the public announcement of the practice of polygamy, and the more recent accusations leveled by W. W. Drummond.

Brigham responded to news of the incoming army by declaring martial law. The following year, to protect the Saints, he directed them to evacuate Salt Lake City and go south to Provo. Fearing the soldiers might destroy what work had been done on the Salt Lake Temple, Brigham ordered people to bury the foundation. To allow time for a mediator to arrive and try to work out a peaceful resolution, President Young asked the Nauvoo Legion to slow down the army by harassing them.

The Nauvoo Legion and "Mormon Raiders," such as Lot Smith, Ephraim Hanks, and Porter Rockwell, were so successful in running off the army's cattle, burning forage for the army's animals, and capturing wagon trains of supplies that the army was forced to spend the winter of 1857–1858 in Fort Bridger. The Mormons had burned this fort earlier so the army would not be able to use it against them.

In September of 1857, Captain Stewart Van Vliet of the United States Government arrived in Salt Lake City to interview government leaders and to arrange to purchase supplies for the incoming troops. When Captain Van Vliet interviewed Brigham and other church leaders, they related the history of abuse and neglect they had received from the government, including the severe persecution they had endured in Missouri and Illinois without receiving any redress from the government. At the end of his talks, Captain Van Vliet concluded the Mormons were not in rebellion. He then went to Washington, accompanied by the Utah delegate, John M. Bernhisel, to inform Washington of the results of his investigation.[21]

After serving in Congress for ten years, John M. Bernhisel returned to Salt Lake City in 1863. He was sixty-four years old when he asked Brigham Young to allow him to retire from public service. John then resumed his medical practice and for the next eighteen years was a familiar and esteemed figure in medical and business circles. On 16 February 1864, Dr. Bernhisel was elected president of the Salt Lake Board of Examination of Physicians.

John M. Bernhisel died in Salt Lake City on 28 September 1881. The Saints greatly mourned the loss of this respected doctor and astute politician. The Deseret News said of John: "He was an intimate friend of the Prophet Joseph Smith and was universally respected and beloved for his integrity and many noble virtues. He was a man of intelligence and education, and was the first Delegate from Utah to the Congress of the United States. He lived a long and useful life and died firm in the faith of the Everlasting Gospel."[22]

Notes

1. B. H. Roberts, ed., *History of the Church of Jesus Christ of Latter-day Saints*, Period 1, vol. 5 (Salt Lake City: Deseret Book Company, 1950), 414.

2. Eugene E. Campbell, *Establishing Zion: The Mormon Church in the American West, 1847–1869* (Salt Lake City: Signature Books, 1988), 205.

3. Glen Barrett, "Dr. John M. Bernhisel, Mormon Elder in Congress," *Utah Historical Quarterly* 36 (1968), 159.

4. Leonard J. Arrington, *Brigham Young, American Moses* (Urbana: University of Illinois Press, 1986), 227.

5. Campbell, *Establishing Zion: The Mormon Church in the American West, 1847–1869*, 207.

6. Gene A. Sessions, *Mormon Thunder, A Documentary History of Jedediah Morgan Grant* (Urbana: University of Illinois Press), 87.

7. Campbell, *Establishing Zion: The Mormon Church in the American West, 1847–1869*, 210–11.

8. John Henry Evans, *The Story of Utah, The Beehive State* (New York: The Macmillan Company, 1933), 106.

9. *Journal of Discourses*, 26 vols. (London, 1854–86), 187.

10. Arrington, *Brigham Young, American Moses*, 230.

11. Campbell, Establishing Zion, *Establishing Zion: The Mormon Church in the American West, 1847–1869*, 219.

12. Arrington, *Brigham Young, American Moses*, p. 233.

13. Andrew Love Neff, *History of Utah, 1847–1936*, Leland H. Creer, ed. (Salt Lake City: Deseret News Press, 1940) 177.

14. Campbell, Establishing Zion, *Establishing Zion: The Mormon Church in the American West, 1847–1869*, 224.

15. Ibid.

16. Ibid.

17. *Journal of Discourses*, 26 vols. (London, 1854–86), 183.

18. Utah was not admitted as a state until 1896.

19. Arrington, *Brigham Young, American Moses*, 238.

20. Ibid., 248.

21. *Journal History of the Church of Jesus Christ of Latter-day Saints*, 15 September 1857, (Salt Lake City: LDS Church History Library).

22. "Dr. Bernhisel is Dead," *Deseret Evening News*, 28 September, 1881.

James S. Brown

1828–1902

"Look at that fire," Tabate bellowed at Elder James S. Brown, pointing at the roaring fire. "It is made to consume the flesh off of your bones!"[1] Surrounded by angry men, curious onlookers, and a few fearful members of the Church, Elder Brown did as he was told and looked at the flames. However, this did not strike fear into his heart like Tabate hoped it would. Instead, Elder Brown felt the sweet presence of the Holy Spirit.

James S. Brown had come to the Society Islands in the fall of 1849. At first, authorities had refused to allow the missionaries to preach. James spent his time learning the language until the missionaries were given permission to preach. Elder Brown traveled to various small islands and in December, arrived in Raivavai, where there were eight members of the Church.

Problems arose when Elder Brown baptized a few new converts. Upset by the conversions, tribal leaders held a council to determine how they could get rid of Mormonism and the "American Plant," as they called Elder Brown. James wrote: "Some proposed to fasten the 'the plant' on a log, tow it out to sea, where the sharks would eat it, while others suggest burning or making a roast of me."[2]

Council members were swayed by those who were hostile to the Mormons and they decided to give Elder Brown two options—either leave the island or be killed. When someone hurried to tell Elder Brown of their decision, he hurried to the council meeting, thinking to allay their concerns and persuade them to change their minds. Instead, pandemonium erupted. He relates, "My presence, instead of having a conciliatory effect, created the wildest confusion." A heavy-set man named Tabate charged the missionary, shouting, "I will slay you!"[3]

A few men restrained Tabate, allowing Elder Brown to leave in safety. Elder Brown's efforts had not been in vain, and the council reversed their decision and allowed him to stay.

As time went on, Elder Brown was able to baptize twenty new members. Councils were held occasionally to see what could be done about ridding the island of the American Plant, but the new converts managed to stop the council from taking any harsh actions.

However, emotions flared anew when an important chief requested that his granddaughter—his direct heir—be baptized. The natives were so enraged by this that the chief called an island-wide meeting so that his granddaughter, Teraa, could tell the crowd that it was her own decision to be baptized, and it had nothing to do with Elder Brown's undue influence.

Aggrieved feelings from this incident had not yet faded when ministers of another faith came to the island and made inflammatory speeches against Mormonism. Among other things, the ministers told the natives that they had admitted a wolf into their fold and that if they did not get rid of Elder Brown, the ministers would leave and not return. As the ministers were very well-liked, this caused great anxiety and distress among the natives. It was decided to hold a council meeting in May of 1852, where they would determine Elder Brown's fate, once and for all.

Word spread quickly on the small island, and the night before the special council, the natives began to gather, bringing fruit, fish, and poultry for a feast. That night, the natives ate, sang, danced, and argued about Mormonism. James wrote, "They kept up a continual howl all the night long, firing their guns, singing their war songs, and burning their campfires. While this was going on, we held prayer and testimony meeting, never sleeping a moment the whole night. Many times we could hear the crowd outside boasting."[4]

Some of the natives were so openly hostile to the Mormons that they gathered together in one home for safety. Elder Brown and other church members held a night-long fast and testimony meeting while men outside their hut chanted war songs, fired guns, and made a bonfire from the fence they tore down that had enclosed the house.

In the morning, two strong men carrying clubs came to escort Elder Brown to the council meeting. As he walked between his guards and stood before the assembly of chiefs, James recalled the promise President Brigham Young had given him prior to his leaving on this mission.

"He told me, in the name of the Lord God of Israel, that though men should seek my life, yet I should return in safety, having done good and honor to myself and the Church and the Kingdom of God."[5]

Fifteen athletic young men stood near the large bonfire as Elder Brown faced the council. Tabate, the leader of the group who wanted to get rid of the Mormon missionaries, turned to the crowd and ordered, "All the Britons stand on the right hand with the sheep and the Mormons stand on the left where the goats are."

Two faithful members, Rivae and his wife, who was cradling her eight-month old baby in her arms, stepped forward. They knew what Tabate wanted to do. "If you burn this man," Rivae announced, pointing to Elder Brown, "you must burn me first."

His wife also spoke up. "I am a Mormon and this baby will be a Mormon if he lives, so you will have to burn all of us to put a stop to Mormonism."[6]

Tabate ordered them to stand aside and began listing the charges against Elder Brown, telling the council that the missionary had deliberately and maliciously led the people astray. When Elder Brown tried to speak, one of the chiefs told him that the decision had already been made to burn him to death.

That was when Tabate told Elder Brown to look at the fire, telling him that it had been made "to consume the flesh off of your bones!"[7]

At that precise moment, Elder Brown felt the promptings of the Spirit. Raising his arms in the air, he declared, "In the name of Israel's God, I defy the host of you, for I serve that God who delivered Daniel from the den of lions and the three Hebrew children from the fiery furnace!"[8]

A few natives shouted that Elder Brown should be thrown into the fire, but those closest to him were afraid to touch the missionary. After being urged on by others, some of the younger men went to grab Elder Brown, but they were unexpectedly stopped by other men. Fighting broke out and in the ensuing melee, people slipped away. In the end, Elder Brown and other members of the Church were allowed to return to their homes, and the bonfire was left to burn itself out.

Elder Brown said that in the days that followed, a different feeling— one of peace—pervaded the village. Quietly, Elder Brown went about his labors.

One day, Elder Brown saw one of the men who had wanted to kill him that fateful night. When the man happened to turn, he appeared startled and took off running.

Curious, James ran after him. Catching up, he grabbed the man's arm and asked, "Why do you run from me?"

"Your God is a God of power and I was afraid to meet his servant," the man admitted, saying he had received a spiritual manifestation when Elder Brown had defied the council that night.

He related, "At the moment that you defied us, there was a brilliant light, or pillar of fire, bore down close over your head. We thought you had prayed to your God and that he had sent that fire to burn us and our people if we harmed you. The young men did not see the light. They were going to burn you and we tried to stop them. So we got into a fight. Now we all know that you are a true servant of God, and we do not like to meet you, out of fear."

James assured the man he meant no harm to anyone. All he wanted was to share the good news of the gospel. Elder Brown stated, "I was treated with great respect ever afterwards. . . . A feeling of quiet and safety pervaded the village, especially in and about our residence, such as we had not before known on the island."[9]

James Stephens Brown proved himself a loyal and faithful member of the Church not only on that mission but also during his entire life. James was born on 4 July 1828 in Davidson, North Carolina. His family were settlers. Living on the fringe of civilization, James was used to danger and often faced peril from outlaws, wild beasts, and Indians. He learned early how to shoot a gun and use a tomahawk. Although nearly everyone in the area felt that all Mormons ought to be shot or burned at the stake, James and his family didn't. They even went to listen to a Mormon missionary, Jacob Pfoutz, who came to the area to share the gospel message. Jacob's preaching had quite an effect on young James, who said, "As to myself, it seemed that I had not only heard it thunder, but I had seen the lightning and felt it through every fibre of my system, from the crown of my head to the soles of my feet."[10]

James and his family were living in Nauvoo when the Saints were expelled from that city. Undaunted about the prospects of undertaking a journey of a thousand miles into an unknown wilderness, James declared that where the Mormons went, he would go and where they died, he would die.[11]

James had traveled to Iowa with the Saints when President Brigham Young arrived, asking the people to raise a battalion of 500 men. James reported that Brigham was determined to raise a battalion and said the Prophet told the Saints that if the young men would not enlist, the middle-aged and old men would, and that a battalion would be raised if it took the Twelve Apostles and the High Priests.[12]

Though he was underage, James enlisted along with his uncle, Alexander Stephens. And while there had been concerns that they might have to fight the Indians and Mexicans, his company had no trouble with them; however, he was often tired and footsore and suffered from lack of water. James recounts:

> So far as I can remember, it was between January 23 and 27, 1847, that we passed over a battlefield where General Kearney and his little command had fought and beaten the Mexicans. There lay broken swords and firearms, and dead horses and mules; and there also were the graves of the slain, while all around the blood-stained soil was plainly within our view. . . .
>
> Here came to our minds the words of President Brigham Young, in his farewell address to the battalion, in which he said: 'You are going into an enemy's land at your country's call. If you will live your religion, obey and respect your officers, and hold sacred the property of the people among whom you travel, and never take anything but what you pay for, I promise you in the name of Israel's God that not one of you shall fall by the hand of an enemy. Though there will be battles fought in your front and in your rear, on your right hand and on your left, you will not have any fighting to do except with wild beasts.[13]

When James was discharged in July 1847, he stayed in California for a time, mining for gold, and was at Sutter's Mill when gold was discovered there. He then went to Salt Lake City, arriving on 28 September 1848. James said that upon his arrival, he and other members of the battalion were welcomed in royal style by Presidents Brigham Young and Heber C. Kimball.

In September of 1849, President Young asked Elders James S. Brown,

Addison Pratt, and Hyrum Blackwell to go on a mission to the Society Islands. It was during this mission that Elder Brown had the harrowing experience of nearly being burned to death.

When President Young personally called James to this mission, the Prophet asked, "Brother James, will you go?"

Elder Brown replied, "I am an illiterate youth, cannot read or write, and I do not know what good I can do; but if it is the will of the Lord that I should go, and you say so, I will do the best that I can."

Brigham Young then sat down next to him and, placing his right hand on James's left knee, said, "It is the will of the Lord that you go, and I say go; I am not afraid to risk you. And I promise you in the name of the Lord God of Israel that if you go you will be blessed, and do good, and be an honor to yourself and to the Church and kingdom of God. Although men will seek your life, you shall be spared and return to the bosom of the Church in safety."[14]

While on this mission, James and the other elders were faced with many challenges. Besides learning a difficult language, they sometimes lacked food. James wrote, "Food had become very scare, so that we had to eat seasnails, and bugs that played on the surface of salt water pools. These bugs were about the size of the end of a man's thumb . . . yet when a man has gone long enough without food, they become quite tempting, and he is not very particular about the legs, either."[15]

When other sources of food failed, the natives would go to the fresh water straits and find creatures that resembled young snakes. These creatures were from six to ten inches long and had a snake's mouth and a spinal column. James reported that when these creatures were boiled in saltwater or hung over the fire, they would squirm a moment or two, then "they were ready for the missionary's meal, taken without pepper or salt." James explained that when he ate one, he would grab the snake by the head, take hold of the body with his teeth and slide his teeth along the body to strip off the flesh, continuing until he reached the head and all the meat was gone.[16]

James S. Brown arrived home from this mission on 22 May 1853, after being gone three years and eight months. James wrote, "On the 23rd, I called at President Brigham Young's office and reported myself and mission. He received me very kindly, and welcomed me home again."[17]

During the October General Conference in 1853, Brigham Young announced the Church was starting a series of Indian missions. At the close of conference, Elder Orson Hyde read the names of thirty-nine men who had been selected to participate in the newest colonizing expedition to the Indians. James Brown was selected to be one of the leaders and was told to be ready to leave in ten days.

The purpose of the mission was to "build an outpost from which to operate as peacemakers among the Indians, to teach civilization to them, to try to teach them to cultivate the soil, to instruct them in the arts and sciences if possible, and by that means prevent trouble for the frontier settlements and the immigrant companies."[18]

The missionaries spent the winter at Fort Bridger. It was a hard winter and they used their time to learn the Shoshone language. When hungry Indians, looking starved, came to the fort, the missionaries divided what little food they had. In the spring, the men began to plow the land and plant crops, having lived for many weeks on bread and water.[19]

In mid-April, James S. Brown, James Davis, Elijah Ward, and Isaac Bullock, the leader of the group, went to meet with Chief Washakie. When the elders mentioned that they were going to visit the Shoshones, the chief said that he had heard there were bad men there, but since they wished to go, would provide them with a guide.

They set off, with the guide riding far ahead of them. After twenty miles, the guide disappeared, making the missionaries feel very uneasy. Reaching the top of a hill, they saw an Indian camp with thousands of Indians beating drums and singing war songs in preparation for battle. It was impossible to leave undetected, so the missionaries rode into camp. A chief came out to meet them. He was polite, but cold. He ordered others to take care of the missionary's horses, and then offered them food. When they went into his lodge, the chief's demeanor changed, and he became friendlier. He told them that they could use his lodge since he was leaving. The chief said he was fearful for his safety, as there were men in the camp he could not control.[20]

The missionaries were in a challenging situation. James said, "There we were surrounded by three hundred Indian lodges, and between fifteen hundred and two thousand Indians.... It was dark, our horses had been taken away, we knew not where, and we were between four and five hundred miles from any source of protection.... The chief had confessed his inability to control some men in his camp, and had acknowledged that he was afraid to stop in his own lodge, he and his family seeking safer quarters. We were also without food, and the showdown of death seemed to hover over and close around us, while the war song and dance were heard plainly. . . . Then what should we do? Put our trust in God, and go to bed, and if we were killed we wouldn't have far to fall."[21]

Just when it seemed things could not get any worse, they did. The next day, L.B. Ryan, the leader of a band of desperadoes and a man who had sworn vengeance on the first Mormons he met, rode into camp.

When told about the white men, Ryan entered the missionary's lodge with seven young warriors, all of them armed with Colt revolvers, as well as bows and arrows. When Ryan asked what they were doing there, Elder Bullock informed him that they were from Utah and were getting acquainted with the Indians—to see about the possibility of trading goods and to see what resources the land had to offer.

As they talked, James unobtrusively pulled out his bowie knife and placed his gun nearby. The other missionaries did the same. Their actions did not go unnoticed, and after a few meaningful looks at the men and their weapons, Ryan and his men left.

James and the others knew that if Ryan came in again, it would be to massacre them, so they readied themselves the best they could. They thought about trying to locate their horses so they could leave, but the Spirit seemed to tell them not to attempt it. Outside their lodge, the dancing, shouting, and singing continued on as it had the day before. That night, the missionaries went to bed fully dressed, with their boots on.

The following day, in the afternoon, the chief returned—bringing their horses. With a slight nod, he indicated that they should leave. As they mounted their horses, Ryan and his associates came up and asked what route they proposed to take back to Utah. Elder Bullock told him. The elders had gone only a short distance when suddenly, the chief appeared ahead of them on the trail. He warned them not to return the way Elder Bullock had said, informing them that Ryan and a group of Indians were planning on ambushing them.

Inexplicably, Elder Bullock insisted on returning the way he had said, feeling that not doing so would mean he had lied to the Indians. Although James and the other missionaries felt it meant certain death, they decided to stay with Elder Bullock. A short time later, it began to rain heavily, and although the precipitation made traveling uncomfortable, the elders were glad for the rain, which would obliterate their tracks. They also traveled in the creek bed to make it even harder for Ryan and the others to track them. When they left the creek, they made their way through the rocky cliffs, and by so doing, were able to escape.[22]

When the missionaries arrived in Green River, Utah, the townspeople gladly supplied their needs. James said that they knew the missionaries had been sent by Brigham Young to protect people like them, as well as innocent immigrants and their property, from Indian raids and from the more wicked, white desperadoes.[23]

James stayed in Green River for a time, acting as an interpreter. He said that rough men were constantly coming into town. "They would camp a day or two on the river, and drink, gamble and fight . . . the traders and rough mountain men . . . were numerous . . . [and] sometimes there would be a perfect jam of wagons and cattle, and two or three hundred men. There were quarrels and fights, and often men would be shot or stabbed . . . it was almost impossible for the sheriff or any other officer to serve a writ or order of court, unless he had a posse to back him."[24]

In July 1854, James was at Fort Bridger when Porter Rockwell brought him a license from Brigham Young, which authorized him and Porter to trade with the Indians. That August, James accompanied Brigham Young on a trip to Chief Catalos and his band of Shoshones, acting as an interpreter. Brigham gave the Shoshones a number of gifts, talked about friendship, and said he would leave other goods with James so he could trade with them. James said that Brigham "also advised them [Shoshones] to be good people and to live at peace with all men, for we had the same great Father."[25] After listening to Brigham's message, the Indians said that their hearts felt good and they parted with good feelings.

James went north and traded with the Indians in Ogden until Brigham asked him to go to another band of Shoshones that winter. Brigham sent a letter with James, asking him to read it to the Indians. After hearing President Young's message, the Shoshones said they felt better about getting along with the settlers. James continued to teach and preach and in December, opened a school and taught a group of thirty men the Shoshone language.

At General Conference held on 6 April 1855, James was once again called to go preach to the Indians. After providing for his family, James went to Salt Lake City where he met with other missionaries. He said, "I was appointed by President Brigham Young to take the presidency of the mission among the Shoshones. . . . I set out on May 8, 1855, in company with four other Elders."[26]

After arriving in Green River in June, the missionaries traveled north to the Shoshone, Bannock, and Flathead territories, and then went south-east to Elk Mountain and the Moab area. Finally, they went southwest to Las Vegas, and from there, west to White Pine and Carson Valley. As they talked with other Indians, the missionaries learned that the Crow and Blackfeet Indians were very hostile toward them.

One morning, James startled awake from a vivid dream. In his dream, a large band of hostile Indians came upon them. When he woke, he told the other two men about his dream. The missionaries took it as a warning and packing up quickly, rode to a high bluff, which gave them a good view of the area. Looking down at the spot where they had camped, they saw a group of Indians ride up, just as James had dreamed. Although the elders had escaped temporarily, they were still in Indian country and knew they could not escape detection for very long.

As the Indians valued bravery, they decided their best move would be to ride boldly to the Indian's camp. As they did, James reported, "Soon we were completely surrounded by a score of armed warriors in full cos-tume of war paint; as these closed in their circle, they saluted us with a war whoop." There were approximately three thousand Indians, all well-armed with rifles, revolvers, bows, and arrows. They met with Chief Washakie, who said he and his men had beaten the Crows and Blackfeet in battle the day before and were now hurrying to leave before the Crows and Blackfeet could return with reinforcements.[27]

James told the chief that when they had time, he wanted to read them a letter he had brought from Brigham Young. Although James also carried a Book of Mormon, he was not at all sure they would receive it, since "we could see plainly from their frowns that they were not at all friendly to us."

When the Indians set up camp that afternoon, the missionaries were taken to a lodge. Indian councilors then filed in, each of them shak-ing hands with the missionaries, even though some of them appeared unfriendly. When everyone was seated, the chief said, "Now tell us what you have to say. Tell it straight, and no crooked talk, for we do not want any lies, but the truth."[28]

James said, "With as few words as possible, we told Washakie we had a letter from the big Mormon captain to him and his people." James then translated it, telling the Indians that "President Young had sent us to Washakie and his people as their friends, that we were truthful and good men, who would tell them many good things about how to live in peace with all people; that President Young and the Mormon people were true friends to the Indian race, and wished them to be our friends, that we might live in peace with each together . . . President Young proposed to furnish seed and tools, and some good men to show and help the Indians to put in their crops. The letter further said that after a while, when we understood each other better, we would tell them about their forefathers, and about God; that we had a book that told a great many things regarding the Great Spirit's dealings with their forefathers, and what He would do for them and their children."[29]

James then presented the Book of Mormon to Chief Washakie. The book and a peace pipe passed around the circle of councilors twenty-one times. One of the Indians commented that the book was of no use to them—that they needed supplies, something to help them eat or hunt with—not a book.

Chief Washakie opened the book, turned the pages, then declared:

> You are all fools; you are blind and cannot see; you have no ears, for you do not hear; you are fools, for you do not understand. These men are our friends. The great Mormon captain has talked with our Father above the clouds, and He told the Mormon captain to send these good men here to tell us the truth, and not a lie. . . . They talk straight, with one tongue, and tell us that after a few more snows, the buffalo will be gone, and if we do not learn some other way to get something to eat, we will starve to death. Now, we know that is the truth, for this country was once covered with buffalo . . . but now, since the white man has made a road across our land, and has killed off our game, we are hungry, and there is nothing for us to eat. . . . The Great father had directed "the big Mormon captain" to send these men to us, to talk good talk, and they have talked good, and made our hearts feel very glad . . . They are our friends, and we will be their friends.[30]

A few months later, James baptized the first three Shoshone women that came into The Church of Jesus Christ of Latter-day Saints.[31]

In August 1855, James returned home briefly to attend to his family and help on the farm.[32] While he was home, his family came down with cholera. Despite this, James decided to return to his mission, feeling that if he was obedient and went, his family would be healed. His uncle, Captain James Brown, stopped by as he was preparing to leave and told James that he was coldhearted to leave his family in such a poor condition.

James replied that it was his belief that if he continued his missionary labors, his family would be healed sooner than if he should neglect his duties. Captain James Brown lifted his hands and said, "Jim, you're right. Go ahead, and God bless you. Your family shall be healed, and not suffer. I will go in and pray for them."[33] His uncle blessed the family, and later James learned that they were healed the same hour that he left.

That December, James returned home for the winter to care for his family. He had completely worn out his clothes and only had one old flannel shirt that he had patched together out of two old ones, one pair of buckskin pants, a beaver cap, and a pair of moccasins.

During the winter months, he preached to the Saints and visited the Indians who were camped along the Weber River. Once, while visiting the Indians, he was caught in a snowstorm. Instead of going home as he had planned, he went first to get his cattle out of the canyon. However, the snow was deep and after a while, his horse gave out, leaving James to proceed on foot. He would walk along to break the trail, lead his horse a few rods, then go ahead to break trail again, continuing until he was exhausted.

When James realized he could not make it home that night, he decided to camp in a clump of cottonwood trees. While making camp, James discovered that his matches were wet, along with his extra blanket and clothing.

James said, "For a time, I thought I would die of exhaustion and thirst. I knew that if I ceased to exert myself I would chill to death. Finally it occurred to my mind to tear off a piece of my shirt, roll it up, hold it in one hand, and with my revolver shoot through it and start a fire."[34]

To get water, James took off his heavy leggings, fashioning them into a kind of basin. He then filled the makeshift bowl with snow and put it near the fire to melt. In the morning, James had to break a trail in the snow for his cattle, as they were unable to move. He was able to make it home safely.

In the spring of 1856, James was preparing to return to his mission when he received word that he had been released. Then, in August, he received a letter from Brigham Young, calling him on a thirty-day mission to the Indians in Deep Creep. James said that he and the other missionaries were well-received because many of the Indians had received spiritual manifestations. James wrote that the Indians "claimed to have received dreams and visions, in which heavenly messengers appeared and told them to go into Tooele and call on the Bishops who would tell them what to do, and for them to obey the Bishops. Accordingly, scores of them went to

Grantsville and related their story, when they were told to believe in Christ and repent and be baptized. Many of them obeyed this advice, and then a missionary was sent out and located among them."[35]

Around this time, a Bannock Indian Chief, Snag, and twelve of his prominent men asked James if he would go with them to Salt Lake City to see President Brigham Young. James said, "I accompanied them to President Young's residence, where he received them kindly, furnishing them with necessary supplies of food and fuel."[36] Afterwards, Brigham told the bishops in the northern settlements to supply the Indians' wants as much as they could.

In 1857, Brigham Young learned that the government was sending an army to Utah to put down a supposed rebellion and install a new governor. Brigham immediately alerted the military to prepare themselves to defend the area against invaders. As the militia was organized in various areas in Utah, James was elected captain of the first company of infantry in the Weber district. He and his family, following the order of Brigham Young, moved south temporarily until the matter was settled amicably the following July.

A year later, Brigham asked James to accompany General Horace S. Eldredge and a company of twenty Mormon men to Nebraska. On his return to Utah in June 1859, James was assigned to help a company of 353 people travel across the plains.[37]

In February 1860, James received a letter from Brigham Young, informing him that he was to accompany Apostles Amasa Lyman and Charles C. Rich on a mission to Great Britain the following April. James packed a ham, a change of clothing, and a shot pouch. Carrying his rifle and wearing a new pair of boots, Elder Brown began his journey without a single dollar in his pocket. When he arrived in Salt Lake City to be set apart, President Brigham Young gave the new missionaries some counsel and asked James to take charge of one of the teams. Upon his return to the United States two years later, James was assigned to be the captain and guide for a company of 250 Saints. They arrived in Salt Lake City in September 1862.[38]

Shortly after his return, Brigham told James to move his family to Salt Lake City so he could go on another mission, this time a home mission. Brigham told James, "I don't know of any people on earth that need more preaching to than do the Latter-day Saints at home. We send our Elders out to preach and to gather the people . . . then set those people down here in a new country and leave them . . . and the result is that many of them get discouraged and apostatize; whereas, if the Elders would keep the harness on, and preach to and encourage them, they would stay and make good Latter-day Saints."³⁹

James preached and lectured around the Salt Lake Valley for nearly a year, then in 1863, suffered a terrible accident. James had gone to the canyons to get some lumber when he was accidentally shot in the leg. His leg bone was shattered and for nine months, he lay on his back, unable to move.

James said, "During that time two surgical operations were performed . . . I was reduced to a skeleton, and became so weak I could not feed myself or even lift a sheet of paper."⁴⁰

It took a long time for him to recover but eventually James was able to resume his activities, though he suffered nearly constant pain.

In July 1867, James went with a few men to do some prospecting. One day, their horses strayed. When James went to find them, he stumbled upon a war party of approximately eighty Indians. James rode hard for camp, with the Indians following closely behind. As they approached camp, one Indian drew near enough to begin to draw his bow. James shouted for help and one of the men in camp fired at the Indian, saving James' life. When the conflict was over, three men had been killed and another had, like James, narrowly escaped harm.

During 1868, James began hauling coal from Coalville to Salt Lake City and transporting tithing produce between Ogden and Logan. He was able to do this work even though he continued to suffer painful abscesses in his leg, which had never healed properly from his accident. Finally, in May 1869, his left leg was amputated four inches from the hip.

During General Conference in April 1872, James was called on a mission to the eastern part of the United States. He went, even though he continued to have problems with his prosthetic leg. Unfortunately, the people in Boston were not interested in the gospel. When President George A. Smith released the missionaries, James and the other elders preached their way home.⁴¹

Back in Utah, James began going on preaching tours throughout the state. Then, in September 1875, Brigham Young called James into his office. President Young exclaimed, "Oh Brother James, that I could see you as I have seen you, strong and active! I should like to send you on a mission to those Indians, for you are just the man to go there with a few other good men. The Spirit of the Lord is upon them and they need a few men among them who will teach them the truth."[42]

James told Brigham that he was unable to endure the hardships and exposure that he had previously withstood when he was young because his health had become very poor. Despite being in poor physical condition, James declared that whatever the Spirit of the Lord directed Brigham to ask, he was willing to attempt to the best of his ability and that he was where he had always been—on hand.

President Young replied, "Bless your soul, the Spirit does and had dictated to me all the time to send you to take charge of a mission in that country. You are just the man for it, and if I had sent you before, we would have had a mission and settlements there now."[43]

Brigham directed James to take charge of a mission near the Colorado River and while there, to explore and find sites for new settlements and to build up those new locations. President Young asked James to provide him with a list of good men that could go with him. These men were subsequently called during General Conference in October 1875.

Before he left, James tried to collect on old debts so he could provide for his family during his absence, but times were hard and people were unable to pay him. Although he hated leaving his family with only a ten-day supply of fuel, and less than fifty pounds of flour in the house, James was determined to go on this mission. James blessed his family, telling them that if they would live their religion, they would not suffer.

James went on his mission and did the work he had been asked, even though while he was gone, his artificial leg fell apart. He returned home in 1876. When he went to give Brigham a report of his mission, James said, "If I had been President Young's own son he could not have received me more cordially than he did when I reached his office."[44]

In the fall of 1876, Brigham decided to stimulate the colonization effort. James had only been home one month when the First Presidency sent him once again on a preaching tour to visit various Mormon settlements, lecture on missionary work among the Indians, and recruit volunteers.[45] Because of his poor health and only having one leg, Brigham lent James a team and a wagon, and sent a boy along to help him.

On the way south, James stopped at various settlements to preach and give counsel to leaders. During the trip, James became ill but continued on when he had recovered. As he explored, he would send word back to Salt Lake City after finding a suitable site. Church leaders would then send settlers to colonize the areas that James and his men selected. During his explorations, James traveled hundreds of miles through Navajo land and among the Moquis and the Zunis.

One time, while James and his small company of men were in New Mexico, an Indian stopped to talk to them. He asked the missionaries where they were from and what they were doing. When James replied that they were Mormons, the Indian asked them to come and talk to his people, saying he had heard that the Mormons had the history of their forefathers. He said his people wanted to hear from the Mormons' own lips whether they had such a record and how they came by it.[46]

The missionaries arrived and while they rested, Indians began to gather around. James said, "Almost before I realized it, there were two hundred and fifty to three hundred Navajos there, men, women, and children. My chair was taken out of the wagon, a blanket was spread for me and I sat down, the Indians sitting close around. Two chiefs sat near to him and one said, 'If you have the book of our forefathers, tell us about God and them, and how you came by the book.' "

James pulled out a copy of the Book of Mormon and explained that it was a record of God's dealings with their forefathers, and that the book had been revealed to the Prophet Joseph Smith by an angel. As he told them the story, many Indians had tears in their eyes.

They said, "We know that what you say is true, for the traditions of our good old men who never told a lie agree with your story. Our forefathers did talk with God, and they wrote and when they became wicked and went to war they hid up their records, and we know not where they are."[47]

James said, "At this point the chiefs and about ten other leading men rose up and embraced me, saying, 'Continue to tell us of God and our forefathers, for it does our hearts good to hear of them.' "[48]

In August, James received word that a group of Indians wanted to meet with the "Mormon Chief" and talk about some grievances. The missionaries met with the Indians and agreed to go with them to Salt Lake City so they could talk with Brigham Young. James went along as an interpreter.

After meeting with the Indians, James met privately with Brigham Young and said that unless he was asked, he didn't feel physically capable of returning to his mission. However, when Brigham asked him to preach and get recruits for new settlements, James said he would go. Starting in northern Utah, James began lecturing his way south, stopping at settlements to lecture about the southern mission and to call for volunteers to accompany him to Arizona. Brigham authorized him to take up a collection to support himself and his family so he could continue his missionary labors. James said, "I lectured sixty-five times, and secured about eighty volunteers."[49]

When he arrived back in Arizona, James continued to preach among the Indians. Once, he talked to a chief who was acquainted with Brigham Young. The chief said, "The great Mormon father he talked straight all the time. I think that [is] a good road to travel in. . . . I want to see more of your people. The American's and your people differ in religion. The Mormons say their captain talks with God (Pagocheda) and Americans say God does not talk to men. We do not know what to believe. When God talks to us, then we shall know. Until then we want to live as friends."[50]

This chief invited James to a Navajo religious feast and introduced him to thirteen chiefs and two hundred Navajo Indians. When the Indians asked to go to Salt Lake City to see the Mormons, James made the arrangements. They arrived in Salt Lake City on 29 August 1877.

James went to see President Young, saying, "He was very ill, and I merely called to see him. The great pioneer and prophet who had done so much for the opening up and settlement of the Great West was on his deathbed. The magnificent work of his life was over. In half an hour after I left his room, the noble spirit passed from his body, and he slept in death, awaiting the resurrection morn."[51]

On August 29, the Deseret News reported, "Last evening Elder James S. Brown arrived from the south with a delegation of Navajo Indians. . . . In June last Elder Brown and a party of brethren visited the northeastern Part of Arizona and the northwestern portion of New Mexico. . . . Brother Brown and party held a council with the Indians at the camp of Pal Chil Clane, about two hundred men of the tribe being present on the occasion. . . . The delegation are stopping at the house of Brother Brown, and have been visiting the leading places of interest in the city today."[52]

On August 30, President Daniel H. Wells, counselor to President Young, released James from his mission in Arizona. After President Young's funeral, James accompanied the Indians to Gunnison, and then returned to Salt Lake City. James traveled and lectured among the settlements in Utah, southern Idaho, and western Wyoming, saying he wanted to continue "traveling and preaching in the autumn and winter as President Young had directed me to do."[53]

Then, in March 1892, President Joseph F. Smith visited James at his home and talked about going on another mission to the Society Islands. Although they discussed his poor health, President Smith stated that the First Presidency wanted him to go on this mission. James replied, "I was not afraid to go, as I had faith that God would not require of any man more than he would have the ability to do if he were faithful."[54]

While making preparations to leave, James ran into Apostle Lorenzo Snow, "who told me he felt the spirit of prophecy. He said that the mission I was going on should be one of the greatest I had ever performed; that I would prosper therein and be blessed with more power and influence than ever before. . . . When he [Lorenzo Snow] concluded he took from his pocket two five-dollar gold pieces, remarking that he had been a missionary himself, and insisted that I should take the money, keep it till I got in a close place, and then use it, which I did."[55]

On April 22, President Wilford Woodruff appointed James S. Brown to preside over the Society Islands Mission. James was sixty-four years old, walked on crutches, and had only one leg, since his artificial limb caused such pain that he was unable to wear it. One man, aware of Elder Brown's circumstances, told James that he would not go if he were in such a condition for ten thousand dollars. Despite his poor health, James served in the Society Islands as a mission president for sixteen months and successfully reopened the mission.

Hugh B. Brown wrote of James:

> As a member of the Mormon Battalion he was all that a soldier could be and more than the average man would have been: As a scout and Indian fighter he was brave, and humane and prudent: As a missionary to the South Sea islands he stood true to his post while savage man-eaters were hungering for his flesh. As a husband and a father his course was the same manly, undeviating path of uprightness. He was among those immortal spirits that hewed out this commonwealth and left the impress of their noble lives on the hearts of the people.[56]

Notes

1. James S. Brown, *Life Of A Pioneer: Being the Autobiography of James S. Brown* (Salt Lake City: George Q. Cannon and Sons Company, 1900), 248.

2. Ibid., 240.

3. Ibid., 240–41.

4. Ibid., 246.

5. Ibid., 247.

6. Ibid., 248.

7. Ibid.

8. Ibid., 248–49.

9. Ibid., 251–52.

10. Ibid., 14.

11. Ibid., 117–18.

12. Ibid., 23.

13. Ibid., 73–74.

14. Ibid., 129.

15. Ibid., 158.

16. Ibid., 157–58.

17. Ibid., 315.

18. Eugene E. Campbell, *Establishing Zion, The Mormon Church In The American West, 1847–1869* (Salt Lake City: Signature Books, 1988), 114.

19. James S. Brown, *Giant of the Lord* (Salt Lake City: Bookcraft, 1960), 327.

20. Ibid., 337.

21. Ibid., 338.

22. Ibid., 338–44.

23. Ibid., 348.

24. Ibid., 349.

25. Ibid., 361–62.

26. Ibid., 366.

27. Ibid., 369.

28. Ibid., 371.

29. Ibid., 371–72.

30. Ibid., 372–75.

31. Ibid., 378.

32. At that time, it was normal to allow married men who were called on nearby missions to return home occasionally to take care of heavier farm duties, so their families did not suffer during their absence.

33. Brown, *Giant of the Lord*, 379.

34. Ibid., 388–89.

35. Ibid., 390.

36. Ibid., 395.

37. Ibid., 407–8.

38. Ibid., 425–54.

39. Ibid., 455–56.

40. Ibid., 457.

41. Ibid., 465–67.

42. Ibid., 467.

43. Ibid., 468.

44. Ibid., 474.

45. Leonard J. Arrington, *Brigham Young, American Moses* (Urbana: University of Illinois Press, 1986), 387.

46. James S. Brown, *Giant of the Lord*, 480–81.

47. Ibid., 481–82.

48. Ibid., 482.

49. Ibid., 485.

50. Ibid., 492.

51. Ibid., 493.

52. Ibid., 493–94.

53. Ibid., 494–95.

54. Ibid., 496.

55. Ibid., 497.

56. Ibid., foreword.

Howard Egan

1815–1878

Howard Egan, a rugged and courageous frontiersman, was traveling to the Salt Lake Valley with the Saints when, on the morning of 16 June 1848, he discovered that Indians had driven off a herd of cattle. He immediately alerted William Kimball and T. Ricks, who went with him to retrieve the cattle. It was a dangerous task they faced, since the Indians would be armed and were unlikely to give up the cattle without a fight, but Howard knew that the poverty-stricken Saints desperately needed the cattle.

Howard and his two companions rode hard and were able to catch up with the Indians and the cattle. One of the Indians turned and pointed his rifle at William Kimball. Howard quickly fired his own gun, causing the Indian to miss William, though his horse was hit.

More shots were fired. Then T. Ricks was shot in the back and fell from his horse. Howard shot one of the Indians before he was hit himself in the arm. When other men from camp arrived, the Indians left the cattle behind and retreated. The three men had succeeded in saving the cattle for the Saints.[1]

This experience was one of many as Howard Egan made three trips across the plains, assisting Saints to reach the Salt Lake Valley. Howard Egan was born in Ireland on 15 June 1815. He became a sailor when he was thirteen and married Tamson Parshley when he was twenty-one. He later practiced plural marriage.

Howard joined The Church of Jesus Christ of Latter-day Saints in 1842 and moved to Nauvoo where he worked as a policeman. After proving himself a competent officer, Howard was assigned to guard the Prophet's home. Howard also served a mission to the Eastern States, where he served in the mission presidency.[2]

Howard also served in the Nauvoo Legion, achieving the rank of major. During the exodus of the Saints from Nauvoo, he was put in charge of organizing and moving one hundred families.

While at Winter's Quarters, Howard was asked to take mail to the Mormon Battalion and bring their mail back to their families. This was the first time Howard acted as a mail carrier, but it would not be the last. In coming years, Major Egan would become well-known as a rider for the Pony Express.[3]

On the first trip west, President Young personally asked Major Egan to go with his company and help find a place of refuge for the Saints. Brigham Young's vanguard company left in April of 1847. At the Platte River, Howard worked in water up to his waist all day, helping ferry wagons cross the river. On one calamitous occasion, Howard narrowly escaped drowning after he was thrown into the river when a wagon overturned.

Brigham Young was ill when the pioneers first reached the Salt Lake Valley in July. Howard stayed behind with the Prophet, entering the valley a few days later when President Young was somewhat recovered.[4] Although some of the pioneers were troubled when they saw the desolate valley for the first time, Howard felt nothing but joy. Upon entering the valley, he commented, "My heart felt truly glad, and I rejoiced at having the privilege of beholding this extensive and beautiful valley, that may yet become a home for the Saints."[5]

Constructing a fort and homes were the pioneers' top priorities. Howard helped haul logs from the canyon and built homes until he went back to Winter Quarters with Brigham Young in August.[6]

In May of 1848, Brigham organized a second trip to the Rocky Mountains. He asked Howard to help escort a large company that consisted of over six hundred wagons—the largest company yet to set out for Utah.[7] It was during this trip that Howard was shot when he and his two friends tracked down the stolen cattle.

"When Brigham needed a man he could trust, he called on Howard Egan. Egan made several trips with wagon and teams to the States to bring immigrants into the valley and to haul some needed items such as a printing press, mail, or produce for the church."[8]

In 1849, Howard was asked to carry the mail east and on his return, pilot a third company of Saints across the plains. While making preparations for this trip, the leaders of the Eastern Branch of the Church, Orson Hyde, George A. Smith, and Ezra T. Benson, approached Howard with a problem. Brigham had asked them to send a printing press to Salt Lake City but they had been unable to find wagons big enough to carry the press and someone they could trust to take it to the valley.

Elders Hyde, Smith, and Benson knew that Howard had crossed the plains twice and was familiar with the difficulties inherent in such a journey—including how to deal with hostile Indians, buffalo herds, stampedes, sickness, wolves, and dangerous river crossings. They all felt that Howard Egan was the man to safely transport the printing press.[9]

Howard accepted this assignment, leaving in May 1849. His job was to carry the mail, safeguard the press, and supervise twenty-two wagons and fifty-seven people. Along the trail they passed shallow graves of those who had died along the way, dead cattle that had been poisoned, and heard persistent rumors of deadly attacks on merchant trains and Mormons. Howard checked out each rumor and when the reports were substantiated, called a forced march and traveled night and day until the pioneers were out of danger.[10]

One night, Howard camped by the Platt River in a place he thought was safe. A few hours before daylight, he was woken by a strange rumbling sound. Howard soon realized it was a stampede.

"He jumped out of bed and into his boots, buckled on his belt which carried his Colts pistol and knife, grabbed his hat and left camp on the run to head off the frightened animals. . . . It was so dark that you could not have seen your hand a foot from your face. . . . When running at top speed he ran up against [an] . . . Indian breast to breast."

After running into each other, Howard and the Indian rebounded apart. Howard dropped low, pulling out his gun with his right hand and his knife in his left. He listened carefully but could hear nothing but the animals running. Howard continued on to the river. He did not see any more

Indians, but when daylight came, saw their tracks in the dusty road."[11]

After arriving back in Utah, Howard accepted an offer to lead a company of forty-niners to California. The following year, he returned to Salt Lake City and built a home. As a well-known guide and mountaineer, Howard often drove cattle to California for two men, Livingston and Kinkead, whenever he was not fulfilling assignments given him by Brigham Young.

"The early years of Egan's resident in Salt Lake Valley were taken up with errands done for President Brigham Young, with his trips to California for Livingston and Kinkead, and with his own personal business."[12]

To support his family, Howard bought his own animals, fed them during the winter, and then drove them to California in the spring to sell. He spent part of each trip exploring uncharted areas.

In 1851, Howard returned home from one of his trips to discover that his wife had been seduced by a man named James Monroe and had borne a child from that illicit union. Howard killed the man, and then turned himself into the authorities. He stood trial and was later acquitted.[13]

While driving cattle to California, it was Howard's practice to count the animals every morning. Usually one or more were missing. If too many were gone, Howard would send men to search for the missing cattle. If only a few were gone, he wouldn't bother. On one trip, Howard and his companions were camped near the Malad River when they woke to find a number of cattle missing. Howard went back to look for missing animals. His son tells the story of what happened next: "He climbed a steep ridge . . . [and] saw what he first thought to be the tail feathers of a bird, but in looking a little closer with his field glass he saw that there was an Indian under those feathers."[14] The Indian was preparing to shoot the nearest steer, but when Howard pulled his gun and yelled, the Indian dropped his bow and arrows.

Howard holstered his gun and motioned for the Indian to follow him to camp. He put a guard over him, and then gave him food and blankets. The next morning Howard gave him breakfast and some flour and bacon to take with him and said he was free to go.

Around noon, Howard noticed six head of cattle missing. When he went back to look for them, he saw the same Indian, with two others. Howard held up six fingers, pointed at the cattle, and then over the country. When the Indians left, Howard decided not to pursue the cattle.

That afternoon, Howard and his men saw a cloud of dust. Soon, the three Indians he had seen that morning rode up, bringing in fifteen cows. There was no need to have his men guard the stock at night, as the Indians watched over them from sundown to sunrise. Near the end of the trip, Howard killed three cows and gave them to the Indians. The following year, as he was making another trip to the California market, the same Indians returned and guarded the cows for him at night. At the end of the trip, the first Indian, Tecumseh, decided to stay with Howard.[15]

Although Howard enjoyed his travels, the days were long and often fraught with danger and hardship. In one journal entry, Howard wrote about an arduous ten-day trip he took to California in 1855. He said that while traveling through a trackless and desert country, he "stopped at a brackish spring to get supper, about two hours, and then went on again. . . . We camped about 4 a.m. and started on at 5 o'clock, stopping to breakfast at 9 o'clock. . . . The morning was cold and cloudy. . . . We saw a large Indian camp in the valley. It commenced raining about dark. . . . We started at 6 o'clock in the morning and met the Indians coming up the canyon on our trail. We stopped in the Humboldt valley at 2 p.m. to feed for an hour, and then started at 3 o'clock and traveled until 4 o'clock the next morning without water."[16]

Howard Egan was one of those hardy men who blazed trails from Salt Lake City to California during 1849 and 1861. In time, there were three main routes travelers took when traveling west. One of them, a trail Howard had blazed, was known as "Egan's Trail" and became the preferred route for travelers, as grass and water were fairly plentiful.[17] During 1860–1861, Egan's Trail became part of the route taken by the Pony Express.[18]

In 1857, President James Buchanan ordered an army to Utah to put down a supposed revolt by the Mormons. Brigham Young asked Howard Egan, Lot Smith, and others to guard mountain passes and destroy wagon trains of provisions before they could reach Johnston's Army. On at least one occasion, Howard was sent to California to bring a load of ammunition to Salt Lake City to use in the Utah War, as it was called, in case it was needed.[19]

The following year, shortly after Howard returned from California, the Utah War was settled amicably, largely through the efforts of Brigham's friend, Colonel Thomas L. Kane. Colonel Kane was able to persuade the new Governor, Alfred Cumming, and a few officials to come to Utah. After their arrival, Governor Cumming told Brigham that army officers had warned him that the Mormons would try to poison him. To reassure the governor that their food was safe, Brigham Young asked Howard Egan and Elder Staines to eat at the same table and partake of the same food.[20]

When the Utah War was over, Brigham Young asked Howard Egan and five other men to escort Colonel Kane back east to his home in Philadelphia. However, once they had arrived in Florence, Nebraska, Colonel Kane dismissed them all except Howard, who traveled with Colonel Kane until he had reached his home in Philadelphia. Howard then accompanied the colonel to Washington D.C.[21]

After his return to Utah, Howard Egan was hired as a mail agent. He soon made a name for himself because of his exceptional speed, stamina, and diligence. Once, Howard wagered that he could ride a mule to California in ten days. With 650 miles to cover, few people thought it could be done, but Howard's skills served him well and he won the contest.[22]

Because Howard had proven that he was able to deliver the mail on time, despite the myriad difficulties that inevitably occurred, he was appointed as Superintendent of the Overland Mail Company. He served in this position until the advent of the railroad in 1869.[23]

At that time, mail often was several months old before it could be delivered because it was transported in slow-moving wagons. The Pony Express became so popular because it was a much quicker way of sending and receiving mail. Howard built a Pony Express station at his home in Deep Creek, Utah and when he became superintendent of the Overland Mail Line, this station was used as its headquarters. It was also used as a stopping place for stage coach travelers and emigrants.

As an officer in the Pony Express, Howard had jurisdiction over the Utah route and decided to be the Pony Express rider that carried the mail on the historic, inaugural trip to Salt Lake City. Howard set out on his seventy-five mile journey, carrying four bags of mail. His pony was swift, but the night was so dark that it was impossible to see the road.

Howard rode against a strong, north wind that was "carrying a sleet that cut the face while trying to look ahead. But as long as he could hear the pony's feet pounding the road, he sent him ahead at full speed. All went well, but when he got to Mill Creek, that was covered by a plank bridge, he heard the pony's feet strike the bridge and the next instant pony and rider landed in the creek."[24]

Fortunately, neither Howard nor his mount were hurt, and they were soon up and going again. Howard Egan delivered the first Pony Express mail to Salt Lake City on 7 April 1860.

One day, Howard was carrying the mail when he discovered that Indians were nearby. Because of his knowledge of the area, Howard figured out the spot where they were most likely to ambush him. However, because of the rough terrain, he had to pass through that spot unless he wanted to make a long detour of many miles. Howard developed a plan. He then went on, though at a slow pace, watching carefully. At one point, he rounded a bend and saw Indians hiding in the brush. He quickly backed up, pulled out his guns, and then charged forward. "With pistols in hand, firing rapidly, yelling lustily and spurring his horse to its utmost speed, he dashed through the cordon to safety."[25]

Howard became snow blind on one of his trips. It was early spring and as he rode along the trail, the sun reflected brightly off the snow, which had not yet melted. The sun's reflection was so dazzling that it blinded Howard, who was forced to stop and make camp. Unable to stand the least amount of light, Howard bandaged his eyes with tea leaves, but they did not get any better.

After a few days of misery, two Indians stopped by. When they asked what was wrong, Howard pointed to his eyes, explaining that they were sick and asking the Indians to fix them. One of them said he would try. Taking a firm hold on Howard's head, the Indian pushed the bandage out of the way and started sucking at one of his eyes. At first, Howard accepted the unorthodox treatment, but when it continued, tried to push the Indian off, thinking that the man was going to suck out not only his eye but his brain as well.

The Indian refused to stop, even when Howard began shouting. Howard had just decided his only alternative was to start choking his benefactor when the Indian released him.

Stepping back, the Indian spat out blood, then asked Howard how he felt. Howard replied that the treatment hadn't done much good. The Indian then started sucking on Howard's other eye. Afterwards, his eyes felt a little better, and Howard asked the Indian to repeat the procedure. When he was done, the Indian told Howard that his eyesight would be restored in two days. Two days later, Howard could see again—the snow blindness was gone. Although the treatment had been difficult, Howard said that it completely took away the pain, which up to then, had been very bad.[26]

In the west, travelers of all kinds, including those who drove the Overland Mail wagons, were often attacked by outlaws, desperadoes, and

Indians. On 19 May 1863, Howard was traveling on an Overland Mail wagon when Indians attacked. The driver, W. R. Simson, was shot. As he slumped to the side, Howard grabbed him so he didn't pitch off the wagon. He then grabbed the reins and was able to stop the wagon safely.[27]

While living at Deep Creek, Howard often went to preach to nearby Indians. He had great success. It was recorded that on "June 2, 1874, one hundred Goshute Indians were baptized and here was a general religious movement among them."[28]

During April's General Conference in 1875, Howard was formally called to be a missionary to the Indians.[29] No doubt his success with the Indians at Deep Creek contributed to this calling. Howard worked diligently and was able to share the gospel with a great number of people. Ora Simmons stated that "Major Howard Egan converted three hundred Goshute Indians."[30]

Sometime around 1875, Howard Egan moved to Salt Lake City. He became a Deputy Sheriff and also served as a special guard for President Brigham Young at the Lion House and the Church Offices. After the death of President Young, Howard was appointed to guard the president's grave. A small building was erected so that Howard could look out on the grave any time of the night, without getting out of bed.[31]

After a lifetime of service, Howard Egan died in 1878, at the age of sixty-three. Not only did he defend the Saints and bring them safely across the plains, he was a faithful missionary and peacemaker among the Indians, fulfilling every assignment Brigham Young gave him.

"Egan blazed trails from Utah to California, purchased a partnership in a stagecoach company, was a rider for and managed a division of the Pony Express. His reputation for honesty and dependability, and his respect for the rights of the Indians, won him a prestige seldom equaled then or since. Because of the confidence that the Indians had in him, he was able to preach the Gospel of Jesus Christ to them and to convert many of them."[32]

Notes

1. J. Raman Drake, "Howard Egan, Frontiersman, Pioneer and Pony Express Rider," Master's Thesis, Brigham Young University (copy on file at Salt Lake City: Church Archives, 1956), 94.

2. H. Dean Garrett, ed., *Regional Studies in Latter-day Saint Church History* (Provo: Brigham Young University, 1995), 227.

3. Ibid., 229.

4. Ibid., 229.

5. Drake, "Howard Egan, Frontiersman, Pioneer and Pony Express Rider," 82.

6. Garrett, ed., *Regional Studies in Latter-day Saint Church History*, 230.

7. Ibid.

8. Drake, "Howard Egan, Frontiersman, Pioneer and Pony Express Rider," 2.

9. Ibid., 99–100.

10. Ibid., 103.

11. Wm. E. Egan, ed. and comp., *Pioneering the West, 1846 to 1878, Major Howard Egan's Diary*, (Richmond: Howard R. Egan Estate and Salt Lake City: Press of Skeleton Publishing Co., 1917), 164.

12. Drake, "Howard Egan, Frontiersman, Pioneer and Pony Express Rider," 106.

13. Ibid., 112.

14. Wm. E. Egan, ed. and comp., *Pioneering the West, 1846 to 1878, Major Howard Egan's Diary*, 182–83.

15. Ibid., 183–85.

16. Ibid., 193.

17. Ibid., 195.

18. Drake, "Howard Egan, Frontiersman, Pioneer and Pony Express Rider," 158.

19. Wm. E. Egan, ed. and comp., *Pioneering the West, 1846 to 1878, Major Howard Egan's Diary*, 124.

20. Drake, "Howard Egan, Frontiersman, Pioneer and Pony Express Rider," 125.

21. *Journal History of the Church of Jesus Christ of Latter-day Saints*, 24 August 1858 (Salt Lake City: LDS Church History Library).

22. Drake, "Howard Egan, Frontiersman, Pioneer and Pony Express Rider," 108–10.

23. Garrett, ed., *Regional Studies in Latter-day Saint Church History*, 231.

24. Drake, "Howard Egan, Frontiersman, Pioneer and Pony Express Rider," 148–49.

25. Ibid., 149.

26. Wm. E. Egan, ed. and comp., *Pioneering the West, 1846 to 1878, Major Howard Egan's Diary*, 216–17.

27. Ibid., 260–61.

28. Ibid., 283.

29. *Journal History of the Church of Jesus Christ of Latter-day Saints*, 9 April 1875, (Salt Lake City: LDS Church History Library).

30. Drake, "Howard Egan, Frontiersman, Pioneer and Pony Express Rider," 127–28.

31. Wm. E. Egan, ed. and comp., *Pioneering the West, 1846 to 1878, Major Howard Egan's Diary*, 283.

32. Drake, "Howard Egan, Frontiersman, Pioneer and Pony Express Rider," 1–2.

Jacob Hamblin

1819–1886

Jacob Hamblin led an eventful life as a scout and a colonizer. Under the direction of Brigham Young, Jacob helped settle parts of Utah, Arizona, and New Mexico. However, he is best known for his success as a missionary and a peacemaker among the Indians. Tall and lean, with an unusually relaxed, quiet way of speaking, Jacob had such great success that Brigham Young ordained Jacob Hamblin as an Apostle to the Lamanites.[1]

Jacob Hamblin was born on 6 April 1819, in Salem, Ohio. After he and his wife were baptized, Jacob wanted to go west and join the Saints in Utah. His wife refused to leave but told him to take their three children and go. He traveled to Council Bluffs where he met and married Rachel Judd. Later in his life, he married two more wives.

Mormon historian, John H. Evans, said of Jacob Hamblin:

> Although Jacob Hamblin generally carried a gun of some sort, his dependable weapon was prayer and the most absolute trust in God—a strange and unusual thing in an American scout and frontiersman. And many a time his life was saved from starvation, from the cold, as well as from the Indian arrow by a simple appeal to that source of

power. He ate with the Indians, he slept with them, he talked their language, he prayed with them for the rain to save their crops . . . till he knew more perhaps than any other American ever knew about the natives and exerted far more influence with them. And it is safe to say that no one has ever fought them with a more effective weapon.[2]

Although Jacob was respected and had great influence with the Indians, his life was in danger many times, and perhaps never was he in more peril than during a crisis that occurred during the winter of 1874–1875. At that time, the Navajos were threatening to launch a full-scale war. When Jacob went to their village to try and prevent war, a council was held. The council was a long one and was fraught with tension and high emotions. During one heated exchange, one of the more hostile chiefs threatened to have Jacob stretched out over the fire that was burning in the middle of the lodge. Since he was completely surrounded, Jacob knew it was distinctly possible this threat might be carried out.

This confrontation had its beginnings in a tragedy that took place a few weeks earlier when four young Navajos were caught in a severe snowstorm in Grass Valley. The young men took shelter in a vacant house, but when the blizzard continued to rage, they became hungry and killed a cow. A neighbor heard the shots and, after investigating, informed Mr. McCarty, the owner of the home, that someone was using his house and killing his cattle. McCarty gathered his neighbors and attacked the Navajos, killing three and wounding a fourth, who managed to escape.

Because Mr. McCarty lived in Mormon country, the Navajos thought the depredation had been committed by Mormons. Outraged, the Indians threatened reprisals against all settlers in the area. After being notified about the crisis, Brigham Young directed Jacob to go to the Navajos and tell them that Mormons had not been involved in the murders.

Jacob said, "When President Young heard of it, he requested me to visit the Navajos and satisfy them that our people were not concerned in it. Feeling that the affair, without great care, might bring on a war, I started at once for their country to fill my mission."[3]

Jacob had not been gone long when one of his sons, Joseph, caught up with him and gave him a note from Bishop Levi Stewart. Bishop Stewart told Jacob to return immediately, saying he had just learned from the Paiutes that the Navajos were definitely preparing for war. He told Jacob that President Young did not know the seriousness of the situation or else he never would have asked Jacob to go meet with the Navajos. Bishop Stewart ended by saying that Jacob would surely be killed if he went on.

In response, Jacob declared, "I had been appointed to a mission by the highest authority of God on the earth. My life was of but small moment compared with the lives of the Saints and the interests of the kingdom of God. I determined to trust in the Lord and go on."[4]

Jacob hurried on, hoping to talk with the Navajos before war broke out. Upon his arrival at the Navajo camp, Jacob was disturbed to discover that Chief Hastele, who normally acted as a mediator, was not there. The seriousness of the situation was heightened when Jacob tried to explain about the killings but was curtly told to wait—that he would be allowed to speak later. The Indians told Jacob he would be allowed to speak during a special council that would be held when all of the chiefs had arrived. At that time, the Indians said, they would settle on a course of action.

Jacob waited tensely until the following afternoon when the last of the chiefs finally arrived. Jacob was told to enter the lodge first and take his seat at the far end. Twenty-four Navajos crowded in after him. The council opened by a Navajo spokesman declaring that what Jacob had said about the murders the night before was false. The spokesman said that because the Mormons had encouraged the Navajos to cross the river and trade with them, three of their young men had been murdered and the fourth had suffered grievous wounds. When others spoke, they painted a similarly grim picture, with the blame for the murders being placed squarely upon the Mormons. Finally, Jacob was allowed to talk.

One of Jacob's unique characteristics was that he always spoke in a very low, calm tone of voice. To hear him, one had to pay strict attention. Indians, as well as settlers, were always favorably impressed by his manner of speaking.

First, Jacob spoke about his long association with the Navajos, reminding them that he had never done them a single wrong. He then explained that the Mormons had not killed the young men, but a Mr. McCarty, who was not a member of the Church, even though he lived in Mormon country.

When he was done, other chiefs spoke. The council continued on through the afternoon and into the evening. Finally, the Indians reached a consensus. They offered to avert war by letting the Mormons pay restitution in the form of one hundred head of cattle for each young man that had been killed and fifty for the wounded one.

It was a way to end the dispute, but Jacob refused, telling them that the Mormons would not pay for a crime they had not committed. Many of the Indians, still convinced that the Mormons were to blame for killing the three young men, became angry. One of the Navajo chiefs angrily jumped to his feet, pointed at the fire, and shouted that Jacob would agree to pay if he were stretched over the bed of hot coals.

Jacob remained calm. He went over the facts again, stating that the Mormons were not involved in the murders and saying matter-of-factly, "Let the Americans pay for their own mischief, I will not sign a writing to pay you one hoof."[5]

When a chief asked if he was afraid, Jacob replied that he was not afraid of his friends. That caused another chief to rebuke Jacob. The chief reproachfully declared that Jacob did not have one friend in the entire Navajo nation and that he had caused many of them to mourn. The atmosphere became very tense, with a number of Indians becoming angry and saying they would go to war. Many of them appeared hostile toward Jacob. Since he was penned in at the far end of the lodge, there was no chance of escaping should they decide to carry out their previous threats.

The chief then asked again, "Are you not afraid?"

Jacob answered, "No, my heart has never known fear."[6]

Jacob was allowed to speak again. His tranquil demeanor and calm speech won the Indians' respect. Finally, after more than twelve hours of discussion, the Indians decided not to wage war immediately, but to let the matter go before Chief Hastele, who would then decide what to do. Jacob told the Navajos that he would return in twenty-five days to find out the results of Hastele's investigation. When Jacob returned, Chief Hastele told him that he had fully investigated the matter and that it had been cleared up to the Navajo's satisfaction.

The beginnings of Jacob Hamblin's remarkable ministry to the Indians had its beginnings in a spiritual manifestation he received while living in Tooele. After coming across the plains in 1850, Jacob and his family were personally greeted by Brigham Young, who asked Jacob to go and help establish a new settlement in Tooele.[7]

The settlers in Tooele had many problems with the Indians. One day, Jacob and a group of men went to the canyons to track a band of Indians that had been involved in a series of attacks against the settlers. The men unexpectedly came across the Indian's camp. As they entered with their guns drawn, the chief jumped to his feet. Taking a few steps toward Jacob, the chief began speaking.

Although Jacob was not familiar with the language, he understood that the chief was saying: "I never hurt you, and I do not want to. If you shoot, I will; if you do not, I will not." A strong feeling came over Jacob, which made him want to protect the Indians, not just at that moment, but always. Jacob then had a personal revelation: "The Holy Spirit forcibly impressed me that it was not my calling to shed the blood of the scattered remnant of Israel, but to be a messenger of peace for them. It was also made manifest to me that if I would not thirst for their blood, I should never fall by their hands."[8] This promise was fulfilled many times. Although Jacob's life was frequently in danger, he never harbored a desire to hurt the Indians but always strove for peace and proved himself to be their true friend.

During General Conference in April 1854, twenty-three missionaries, including Jacob Hamblin, were called to serve in the Southern Utah Indian Mission. Apostles Parley P. Pratt and Orson Hyde organized the missionaries, who left Salt Lake City on 4 April 1854. Jacob said, "Taking a horse, cow, garden seeds and some farming tools, I joined in with brother Robert Ritchie and was soon on my way."[9]

Jacob Hamblin, Thales Haskill, Ira Hatch, and a few others established a permanent settlement near the present-day city of Santa Clara. The missionaries began to learn the natives' language, and when possible, taught them the gospel. Their families were allowed to join them. This mission on the Santa Clara River was one of the most important and successful Indian missions in the Church, partially because the elders used a different policy than what Church leaders generally recommended. Although Brigham advised settlers to have no dealings with the Indians except through Indian agents, he told Jacob and the others to associate freely with the Indians. Brigham said that if the elders wanted to have any influence with the Indians, "they must associate with them in their hunting expeditions and other pursuits."[10]

It had always been Brigham Young's policy to treat the Indians fairly, and Jacob did the same. Not only did Jacob visit the Indians, he lived among them, studied their language, played with them, and ate their food. This created a strong bond and once, an Indian boy asked Jacob if he could live with him. Jacob discussed this request with the boy's family. When they gave their approval, Jacob took the boy home and treated him as one of his own children. He later adopted two other Indian children.

Jacob became fluent in several Indian dialects as he worked with the Paiutes, Navajos, and Hopis. Because of his unwavering honesty, bravery, and fairness, Jacob won the Indians' friendship and respect.

In June 1854, Jacob Hamblin and a group of missionaries traveled south to visit different groups of Indians. On their first day, they met a small, friendly band and had an interview with Chief Toquer. Jacob explained that the Mormons had been sent there by Brigham Young to teach the Indians how to farm in a better way and that they wanted to live with them. Jacob told them about The Church of Jesus Christ of Latter-day Saints and explained the principles of the restored gospel. Afterwards, eleven Indians asked to be baptized.[11]

On a second trip a few months later, the missionaries baptized fifty more Indians. By special appointment, Jacob Hamblin was asked to go alone to this group of Indians in November. Brigham also asked Jacob to use his considerable influence to stop the Indians from attacking travelers on their way to California.

A month later, Jacob and a group of missionaries were assigned to establish a permanent settlement on the Santa Clara River. Assisted by the local Indian chief and a tribe of about 800 natives, the missionaries began building log cabins and digging canals so they could irrigate their crops. Although the Indians were already used to growing small patches of wheat, corn, squash, and melons, the missionaries showed them how to cultivate the land more productively. The elders and Indians worked together and at harvest time, shared everything that was raised.

Jacob then asked the Indians to help build a large dam across the Santa Clara River so water could be stored for irrigation purposes. At first, the Indians were reluctant, but when Jacob promised them that if they would help, they would have sufficient water for the crops, Chief Tut-se-gab-its and his tribe worked alongside the settlers to bring rocks for the dam's construction.[12]

They began building in February 1855. The work was hard, and the missionaries were often exposed to the elements during the dam's construction. When Jacob became ill, the missionaries sent for medicine and better food to help him recover more quickly. Once the dam was finished, it was possible for the missionaries and Indians to farm one hundred acres.

However, the Indians were loath to plant corn, saying it would surely dry up and die. Jacob promised the Indians that if they would plant the corn, there would be enough water to raise it. Although they were still skeptical, the Indians planted their seed. When the long, hot days of mid-June arrived, the water in the creek dried up. The Indians reminded Jacob of his promise, saying, "You promised us water if we would help build a dam and plant corn. What about the promise, now the creek is dry? What will we do for something to eat next winter?"[13]

The Indians asked Jacob to pray for rain, saying they believed that if he prayed, the rain would come. Impressed by their faith, Jacob told the missionaries to let the Indians have what little water was left to water their corn.

The next day, Jacob said, "I went aside by myself and prayed to the God of Abraham to forgive me if I had been unwise in promising the Indians water for their crops if they would plant; and that the heavens might give rain, that we might not lose the influence we had over them. It was a clear, cloudless morning, but, while still on my knees; heavy drops of rain fell on my back for about three seconds. I knew it to be a sign that my prayers were answered. I told the Indians that the rain would come. . . . The next morning, a gentle rain commenced falling. . . . We watered our crops all that we wished . . . I think more corn and squash were grown that year, by us, than I ever saw before or since, on the same number of acres."[14]

On 4 August 1857, Brigham Young wrote Jacob Hamblin, saying; "You are hereby appointed to succeed Elder R.C. Allen as president of the Santa Clara Indian Mission. . . . Continue the conciliatory policy toward the Indians which I have ever commended, and see by works of righteousness to obtain their love and confidence. Omit promises where you are not sure you can fill them; and seek to unite the hearts of the brethren on that mission, and let all under your direction be united together in the holy bonds of love and unity. . . . All is peace here, and the Lord is eminently blessing our labors."[15]

Biographer Milton R. Hunter commented on this new assignment, saying, "No better choice than Jacob Hamblin could have been made for the director of the Lamanite Mission. He was without doubt the most influential and successful Mormon missionary to the Indians while Brigham Young was at the helm."[16]

The Mountain Meadows Massacre in September 1857 was a time of great sorrow. Because the perpetrators tried to conceal the truth, there were many years of confusion as to who was involved in the attack. Documents indicate that President Young accepted John D. Lee's account when he claimed that Mormons were not responsible for the tragedy. However, this deception began to unravel when, according to court testimony, Jacob Hamblin went to Salt Lake City, and on 18 June 1858, he told Brigham

Young and George A. Smith that he was certain that Mormons had participated in the massacre.

After listening to Jacob's report, Brigham Young declared, "As soon as we can get a court of justice we will ferret this thing out."[17] It was later discovered that Mormons had been directly involved.

In the fall of 1858, Brigham Young instructed Jacob to take a group of missionaries and visit the Moqui villages in Arizona. Jacob selected ten associates and asked an Indian, Nahraguts, to be their guide. Leaving Santa Clara on October 28, the missionaries were warmly received at the Moqui villages. Jacob appointed four men to stay until spring to learn the Moqui language and to teach the Indians the gospel. This visit was the first of many between Mormons in Utah and the Indians southeast of the Rio Colorado. The exploration of the area by Jacob and other missionaries resulted in the establishment of many Mormon colonies.[18]

Jacob Hamblin traveled constantly among the various Indian tribes, promoting understanding between them and the settlers and resolving disputes before they could erupt into more serious problems. Because Jacob was unfailingly honest in his dealings, the Indians came to have great confidence in him. One example that highlights this trust occurred when Jacob sent his young son, who was also named Jacob, to trade for some blankets at a nearby Indian village.

Leading an extra horse, young Jacob went to the Indians' camp, as he had been directed by his father. He told the chief that his father, Jacob Hamblin, wanted to trade the horse for blankets. The chief agreed and brought out a pile. The boy shook his head, indicating there were not enough blankets. When the chief brought out more blankets, young Jacob agreed to the trade and loaded the blankets onto his pony. When the boy returned home, he showed the blankets to his father, proud to have made such a good trade. Jacob looked at the large number of blankets and told his son that the trade was not fair and that he had to take half of the blankets back.

When young Jacob returned to the Indian village, the chief smiled and said, "I knew you would come back. Jacob Hamblin, your father, he my father, too, and the father of us all." The chief then told the other Indians that Jacob was an honest man and that he had returned the extra blankets.[19]

One of Jacob's goals was to improve the Indians' living conditions. Along with Ira Hatch and Thales Haskell, Jacob taught the Indians various principles of agriculture so they could live off the land and remain in one place without being forced to roam for food. This policy of having the Indians grow their own food was encouraged by Brigham Young and succeeded reasonably well.

Jacob was a passionately religious man whose life's work as a colonizer, interpreter, and mediator, was heavily influenced by his desire to teach people about the gospel. While other frontiersmen carried guns and blasted their way into new western territories, Jacob packed only minimal supplies—a small journal and his treasured Book of Mormon. Time after time, Jacob encountered hostile situations but he always faced them with a profound trust in God. He appeared to be fearless of death, a trait that never failed to impress the Indians and which came from the spiritual revelation he had received in his early years in Utah.

Because Jacob understood the Indian's culture, he was able to look at situations through their eyes. He was able to explain the Indian's thoughts and behavior to the settlers, which improved relationships. Because Jacob had never once lied to or deceived the Indians, they trusted him. Because of Jacob Hamblin, the settlers in southern Utah were spared from many of the wars and attacks that continued to beset other communities in the west.

On 15 December 1876, President Brigham Young ordained Jacob Hamblin to be an Apostle to the Lamanites in St. George, Utah. This action did not mean that he was a member of the Quorum of the Twelve Apostles—it was meant to be a term of great respect bestowed by Brigham upon Jacob for his outstanding service as a missionary to the Indians. One of the main responsibilities of an Apostle was to spread the gospel and Jacob did this with unwavering and steadfast dedication.

In his later years, Jacob continued to work as a peacemaker. He also assisted in locating and establishing various settlements in southern Utah, Arizona, and New Mexico. In 1878, Jacob moved to Amity, Arizona, then four years later, to Pleasanton, New Mexico. Jacob Hamblin died on 31 August 1886.

John R. Murdock, a United States Senator from Arizona said: "Certainly Jacob Hamblin's place in the history of the Southwest and the history of Arizona is that of a trail breaker. He was the trusted agent of President Brigham Young in exploring the intermountain country, establishing Mormon outposts and spying out suitable places for Mormon colonial expansion."[20]

It was said that Jacob might have been a General Authority if he had lived in the Salt Lake Valley, but Hartt Wixom, a biographer, stated that "If Jacob was removed from the frontier, it would not have gotten along without him. The position of Church Presidents Brigham Young and Wilford Woodruff seemed to be: 'Let Jacob continue precisely as he is doing. Help him . . . or stay out of his way.'" Wixom added, "Hamblin easily spent more energy and time in establishing peace between white men and Utah-Arizona Indians than any man who ever lived."[21]

Notes

1. Andrew Jenson, *Latter-day Saint Biographical Encyclopedia*, vol. 3, four volumes (Salt Lake City: Andrew Jenson History Company, 1920), 100.

2. John Henry Evans, *The Heart of Mormonism* (Salt Lake City: Deseret Book Company, 1930), 452–53.

3. James A. Little, *Jacob Hamblin* (Salt Lake City: Bookcraft, 1969), 118.

4. Ibid.

5. Pearson H. Corbett, *Jacob Hamblin, The Peacemaker* (Salt Lake City: Deseret Book, 1952), 354.

6. Paul Bailey, *Jacob Hamblin, Buckskin Apostle* (Los Angeles: Westernlore Press, 1948), 350–64, 70.

7. Corbett, *Jacob Hamblin, The Peacemaker*, 30, 32, 479–480.

8. Ibid., 42.

9. Little, *Jacob Hamblin*, 26.

10. Hunter, *Brigham Young, The Colonizer* (Santa Barbara and Salt Lake City: Peregrine Smith, Inc., 1940), 301.

11. Ibid., 324.

12. Milton R. Hunter, "Jacob Hamblin and the Santa Clara Mission," *Pioneer* vol. 52, no. 1, 2005, 23.

13. Little, *Jacob Hamblin*, 33.

14. Ibid., 33–34.

15. Hunter, *Brigham Young, The Colonizer*, 305.

16. Ibid., 305.

17. B. H. Roberts, *A Comprehensive History of the Church of Jesus Christ of Latter-day Saints, Century I*, vol. 4 (Salt Lake City: Andrew Jenson History Company, 1930), 166.

18. Hunter, "Jacob Hamblin and the Santa Clara Mission," 26.

19. John Henry Evans, *The Story of Utah, The Beehive State* (New York: The Macmillan Company, 1933), 128–29.

20. Corbett, *Jacob Hamblin, The Peacemaker*, 434.

21. Hartt Wixom, *Hamblin, A Modern Look at the Frontier Life and Legend of Jacob Hamblin,* (Springville: Cedar Fort, Inc., 1996), 6, 356.

Ephraim K. Hanks

1826–1896

An angel woke Ephraim K. Hanks, asking him if he would go help the handcart pioneers that had been caught in early snowstorms. Ephraim replied that he would and went back to sleep, but the angel woke him again to ask the same question. He replied affirmatively, but the angel woke Ephraim yet a third time.

Ephraim had stopped to spend the night at the home of a friend, Gurney Brown, when this remarkable manifestation occurred. No doubt the angel had been sent because Ephraim was a skilled outdoorsman and scout and would do his best to complete any assignment given to him.

Ephraim relates his experience:

> Being somewhat fatigued after the day's journey, I retired to rest quite early, and while I still lay wide awake in my bed I heard a voice calling me by name, and then saying: "The hand-cart people are in trouble and you are wanted; will you go and help them?"
>
> I turned instinctively in the direction from whence the voice came and beheld an ordinary sized man in the room. Without any hesitation, I answered "Yes, I will go if I am called." I then turned around to go to

sleep, but had laid only a few minutes when the voice called a second time, repeating almost the same words as on the first occasion. My answer was the same as before. This was repeated a third time. When I got up the next morning I said to Brother Brown, "The hand-cart people are in trouble, and I have promised to go out and help them;" but I did not tell him of my experiences during the night. I now hastened to Salt Lake City, and arrived there on the Saturday, proceeding the Sunday on which the call was made for volunteers to go out and help the last hand-cart companies in.[1]

Ephraim K. Hanks was solidly-built, being six feet tall and weighing two hundred pounds. He was born on 21 March 1826, in Madison, Ohio, and enlisted as a sailor when he was sixteen years old. After being discharged in 1844, he joined the Church. When Brigham needed a strong and fearless leader to protect a company of members as they traveled to Nauvoo amidst much persecution, he asked Ephraim.

When President Brigham Young arrived at Mount Pisgah, Iowa, and asked for volunteers to join the Mormon Battalion, Ephraim was one of the first to join. After serving his time, Ephraim went to the Salt Lake Valley, arriving in July of 1847. He became a member of the Mormon Militia and in 1850, accepted a job carrying mail across the plains. Although being a mail carrier was difficult and often dangerous, Ephraim enjoyed it. During the next seven years, he made the thousand-mile journey over the plains and mountains at least fifty times.

Then came the angelic manifestation in October 1856. Ephraim woke early the next morning and headed for Salt Lake City where he found the city abuzz with the news that the handcart people had been caught in early snowstorms.

During the Sunday session of general conference, Brigham Young stood at the pulpit and said, "I will now give this people the subject and the text for the Elders who may speak [today].... It is this ... many of our brethren and sisters are on the plains with handcarts ... they must be brought here, we must send assistance to them. The text will be—to get them here! ... That is my religion; that is the dictation of the Holy Ghost that I possess. It is to save the people.... I shall call upon the Bishops this day. I shall not wait until tomorrow."

Brigham then went on to explain precisely how many wagons, mules, teams, and teamsters he wanted, as well as how much flour and other supplies they should take. He then declared to the congregation, "I will tell you all that your faith, religion, and profession of religion, will never save one soul of you . . . unless you carry out such principles as I am now teaching you. Go and bring in those people now on the plains. . . . Otherwise, your faith will be in vain. The preaching you have heard will be in vain to you, and you will sink to hell, unless you attend to the things we tell you."[2]

Ephraim was not there to hear Brigham speak, because he and Reddick N. Allred were already on their way to help the handcart pioneers. Then, a blizzard struck. It was so bad that Ephraim, a hardy outdoorsman, declared he had never seen a worse one. The snow became so deep that it became impossible to move the wagons, but Ephraim refused to turn back. He loaded a saddle horse and a pack animal and started out alone.

As Ephraim rode, he happened upon a herd of buffalo. He marveled at this, as it was very rare to find the animals in that area so late in the season. Ephraim was able to shoot and kill one, and then said:

> I skinned and dressed the cow; then cut up part of its meat in long strips and loaded my horses with it. Thereupon I resumed my journey, and traveled on till toward evening. I think the sun was about an hour high in the west when I spied something in the distance that looked like a black streak in the snow. As I got near to it, I perceived it moved; then I was satisfied that this was the long looked for handcart company, led by Captain Edward Martin. I reached the ill-fated train just as the immigrants were camping for the night. The sight that met my gaze as I entered their camp can never be erased from my memory.
>
> The starved forms and haggard countenances of the poor sufferers, as they moved about slowly, shivering with cold, to prepare their scanty evening meal was enough to touch the stoutest heart. When they saw me coming, they hailed me with joy inexpressible, and when they further beheld the supply of fresh meat I brought into camp, their gratitude knew no bounds. Flocking around me, one would say, "Oh, please, give me a small piece of meat"; another would exclaim, "My poor children are starving, do give me a little"; and children with tears in their eyes would call out, "Give me some, give me some."
>
> At first I tried to wait on them and handed out the meat as they called for it; but finally I told them to help themselves. Five minutes later both my horses had been released of their extra burden—the meat was all gone, and the next few hours found the people in camp busily engaged in cooking and eating it, with thankful hearts.[3]

Ephraim then went about the camp administering to the sick. He said,

"Many of the immigrants whose extremities were frozen, lost their limbs, either whole or in part. Many such I washed with water and castile soap, until the frozen parts would fall off, after which I would sever the shreds of flesh from the remaining portions of the limbs with my scissors. Some of the emigrants lost toes, others fingers, and again others whole hands and feet; one woman who now resides in Koosharen, Piute Co., Utah, lost both her legs below the knees, and quite a number who survived became cripples for life."[4]

Ephraim continued:

> After this, the greater portion of my time was devoted to waiting on the sick. "Come to me," "help me" "please administer to my sick wife" or "my dying child," were some of the requests that were made of me almost hourly for some time after I had joined the immigrants and I spend days going from tent to tent administering to the sick. . . . In scores of instances, when we administered to the sick, and rebuked the diseases in the name of the Lord Jesus Christ, the sufferers would rally at once; they were healed almost instantly. I believe I administered to several hundred in a single day; and I could give names of many whose lives were saved by the power of God. . . . I remained with the immigrants until the last of Captain Martin's company arrived in Salt Lake City on the thirtieth day of November, 1856.[5]

There was much discussion about why the handcart pioneers had left so late in the season. Apostle Orson F. Whitney wrote, "Some find fault with and blame Brother Brigham and his council, because of the sufferings . . . on the plains. But let me tell you most emphatically that if all who were entrusted with the care and management of this year's immigration had done as they were counseled and dictated by the First Presidency of this Church, the sufferings and hardships now endured by the companies on their way here would have been avoided. Why? Because they would have left the Missouri river in season, and not have been hindered until into September."[6]

Having gained a reputation as a skilled scout, Ephraim had barely returned from assisting the handcart pioneers when Brigham Young called him to perform another mission: to carry government mail and important messages from Salt Lake City to Independence, Missouri.

That winter was one of the worst ones ever experienced, and it took an expert frontiersman to undertake a journey of this magnitude. It was said of the intrepid Ephraim Hanks, "Few men connected with the Mormon

Church were equal to the task, but President Brigham Young knew who they were."[7]

On the morning of 11 December 1856, Ephraim K. Hanks, along with his good friend, Feramorz Little, received a blessing from the Presidency of the Church, then started east. Near the Continental Divide, a fierce storm struck and the men had to travel in snow that was up to their horses' knees. After going 300 miles, they met freight teams loaded with mail, heading east. Because of delays caused by the snow, the men were low on food. Ephraim told them that he and Feramorz would travel with them and furnish them with buffalo meat.

They had stopped to make camp when Ephraim felt impressed to visit a large tribe of Sioux that were camped nearby in Ash Hollow. When the chief asked who he was, Ephraim said he belonged to the people who had pulled handcarts across the plains and that his chief's name was Brigham Young. Ephraim also told them that Brigham sometimes talked with the Great Spirit.

The chief asked if Ephraim could also talk with the Great Spirit and when Ephraim replied that he could, a few men left the lodge. They returned, carrying an Indian boy who had seriously injured his back when he was thrown from his pony, and was unable to move. The chief asked him to talk to the Great Spirit on the boy's behalf and said that if Ephraim was able to make the boy well, he would be allowed to leave. Ephraim anointed the boy and gave him a blessing, declaring that he would be made whole from that very moment. To the astonishment of all, in a short time, the boy arose and was able to walk.[8]

Ephraim told the Indians that he was escorting a company of freighters and hoped to kill some buffalo for food. The Indians informed him that there had not been any buffalo in that area for months, and because of that, their people were on the verge of starvation. The spirit of prophecy came upon Ephraim and he promised them in the name of the Great Spirit that within three days, the whole country around them would be overrun with buffalo.

When Ephraim returned to his camp, he told the freighters nothing of what had occurred in the Indian's camp. The next morning, about thirty Indians rode up and silently formed two lines, one on each side of the wagons. Ephraim was in the lead wagon and as the wagons passed between them, each Indian moved forward to give Ephraim a bit of choice sausage that had been made from buffalo meat. Ephraim shared the meat, which proved to be a lifesaver to the hungry freighters.

The freighters continued traveling in snow that was almost two feet deep. When they finally arrived at their destination, Ephraim was surprised to see government agents there, buying supplies for Johnston's Army. Ephraim was told that the army was marching to Utah to forcibly put down the Mormon "rebellion" and to replace Governor Brigham Young with a new governor, Alfred Cumming.

Ephraim, Feramorz, and their companions started for Salt Lake City with three wagons loaded with mail. As they passed through Ash Hollow, they met the Indians Ephraim had talked with previously. The Indians told Ephraim that three days after the freighters had left, one of the largest herds of buffalo they had ever seen had come to that part of the country and saved them from starvation.[9]

After Ephraim Hanks returned to the Salt Lake Valley, Brigham Young asked the Utah Militia to try to delay Johnston's Army by harassing them. This was to allow time for a mediator, Thomas L. Kane, to meet with General Johnston and try to negotiate a peaceful settlement. As a captain in the militia, Ephraim took an active part in the Utah War (sometimes called the Echo Canyon War) during 1857 and 1858. According to historian Edward Tullidge, "Scouts and rangers were detailed to perform special duties. Among these were O.P. Rockwell, Ephraim Hanks, and many others."[10]

Ephraim became one of the men known as the "Mormon Raiders," who made daring exploits against Johnston's Army. Once, Ephraim was able to drive off a band of horses and mules. Several times he captured teams, which helped slow the movement of the troops. Solomon F. Kimball said, "Perhaps no subordinate military man, connected with the Mormon Church, played a more important part in the so-called Echo Canyon War during the winter of 1857–1858 than did Elder Ephraim K. Hanks. So daring was he in some of his exploits, that the bravest men in his company were not anxious to follow him on his reconnoitering expeditions."[11]

On one of Ephraim's reconnoitering expeditions, he crawled so close to the army officer's tents that the cook, coming outside at night, unwittingly threw scraps from the general's table on him.[12]

Because of his daring exploits, Ephraim helped keep the leader of the Nauvoo Legion, General Daniel H. Wells, posted on every important movement made by Johnston's Army.

After Thomas L. Kane arrived in Utah, Brigham asked Ephraim to escort him to Fort Scott to meet with General Johnston, Governor Cumming, and other dignitaries. When Thomas was able to persuade the new governor and other officials to go to Salt Lake City and meet with Brigham Young, Ephraim K. Hanks was asked to ride with them and protect the men during the journey. Eventually, a peaceful settlement was reached.

Ephraim then resumed his work delivering and picking up the mail. On one occasion, Ephraim was traveling with Charley Decker when they were caught in a fearful snowstorm and unable to move for twelve days. When their provisions gave out, they discovered that their ammunition had gotten wet, so they were unable to shoot game. Desperate for food, Ephraim displayed amazing bravery in chasing down a buffalo. Solomon Kimball describes the scene: "Eph, possessing a good horse and being a born athlete, chased after a big fat buffalo, ran his horse close to its side, then with both hands grabbed its mane, jumped astride, and while the animal was running at full speed, Eph, with all his might drove his long knife into the buffalo's heart. This thrilling episode over, they jerked the meat and continued their journey."[13]

Occasionally, Ephraim was asked to deliver mail to Fort Laramie. He would load several pack animals and go on his way. On one of these occasions, he was robbed by Indians who took his horse, gun, supplies, and pack animals, leaving him stranded hundreds of miles from home. All Ephraim had, except for the clothes he wore, was a butcher knife and an important letter in an inside pocket. That letter was from Church authorities to the President of the British Mission, which Ephraim had been told to keep separate from the rest of the mail. Ephraim was determined to deliver the letter, and because of his cunning and experience, was able to make his way to Fort Laramie.

After Ephraim retired from this grueling line of work, he began spending much of his time trying to bring about peace between the Indians, settlers, and travelers headed west. Ephraim visited various tribes in troublesome areas, trying to resolve problems as they cropped up. Because of his diplomacy, Ephraim was able to prevent much bloodshed.

Ephraim then set up a trading post east of Salt Lake City at Mountain Dell, where he developed a thriving business keeping a stage station and looking after the Pony Express boys. However, when the road going through Parley's Canyon was completed in 1860, his business fell off. Ephraim then moved to Parley's Park, just north of where Park City is now located, and began raising livestock. While there, Ephraim discovered silver quartz, which led to mining in that area.

In 1865, Ephraim moved back to Salt Lake City. One morning, he was working on building an adobe house when Brigham Young drove up in his carriage. The basement was nearly done and Ephraim was just starting to lay the sun-dried bricks for the wall when Brigham asked, "Ephraim, how thick is that rock wall?" When Ephraim told him it was eight inches thick, Brigham replied, "Tear it all down, Ephraim, and build it twice as thick."

Then, as if to avoid hearing Ephraim's arguments, Brigham drove on. Ephraim had been hauling rock from Ensign Peak for many days, and had already paid a mason to lay the rocks in lime mortar. He dreaded the extra work and expense of doing everything all over again.

The mason, who had overheard the conversation, was rather put out and said, "Brigham Young may be a saint, but he's no kind of a prophet about building stone walls!"

Nevertheless, Ephraim decided to do as President Young had said and told the stone mason to double the wall. The next morning, Ephraim started hauling more rock.

A month later, Ephraim and a few others helpers were laying adobe bricks on the sixteen inch walls when the sky became cloudy. They continued working and as they were putting up the rafters, it began to storm. Rain fell in sheets, causing streamlets of water to run over the unfinished house in all directions. In a short time, the basement of the new house was flooded. However, the sturdy, thick walls remained standing. A few days later, when the water had drained out, the men returned to their work. As they finished laying the rafters, Ephraim drove in his nails to the tune of "We Thank Thee, O God, for a Prophet."[14]

When Brigham Young advised him to buy Lee's Ferry on the Colorado River in 1877, Ephraim sold everything and began making preparations to move. But when Brigham died later that same year, President John Taylor advised Ephraim to go to a different area. Ephraim obeyed, settling first in Burrville, then in Pleasant Creek, Utah.

Ephraim continued to do what he could to promote peace and understanding between the settlers and Indians in the southern part of the state. Because he truly cared about the Indian's welfare and showed it through words and actions, Ephraim had a great influence for good with them. He gave numerous blessings to the Indians, healing many, and in return, they cared for him when he was sick and in need. During his later years, Ephraim served as a Stake Patriarch for Wayne County.

Ephraim K. Hanks died on 9 June 1896. After hearing about his death, the local Indians paid him a touching gesture of respect when they gathered together—one thousand strong—and rimmed the ledges above Ephraim's ranch in silent tribute to their friend and benefactor.[15]

All his life, Ephraim worked vigorously to serve the Lord. Although his life was filled with hardship, he remained true to the gospel at all times. Solomon Kimball paid tribute to Ephraim K. Hanks when he said, "This generation of Latter-day Saints will never fully appreciate what our pioneer boys have done toward the establishment of the Church in these valleys."[16] President Brigham Young loved Ephraim and always spoke highly of him. Once, in talking about Ephraim, Brigham said, "There is a man who has always been ready to lay down his life for the authorities of the Church as well as for the cause of Zion and her people and in due time will receive his reward."[17]

Notes

1. Sidney Alvarus Hanks and Ephraim K. Hanks, *Scouting for the Mormons on the Great Frontier* (Salt Lake City: Deseret Book, 1948), 132–33.

2. *Journal of Discourses*, 26 vols. (London: Latter-day Saints' Book Depot, 1854–86), 113.

3. LeRoy R. Hafen and Ann W. Hafen, *Handcarts To Zion, the story of a Unique Western Migration, 1856–1860* (Glendale; The Arthur H. Clark Company, 1976), 135–36.

4. Ibid.

5. Interview with Ephraim K. Hanks by Andrew Jensen, Church Historian, as found in Sidney Alvarus Hanks and Ephraim K. Hanks, *Scouting for the Mormons on the Great Frontier* (Salt Lake City: Deseret Book, 1948), 139–41.

6. Orson F. Whitney, *Life of Heber C. Kimball* (Salt Lake City: Bookcraft, 1967), 414.

7. Beatrice B. Malouf and Emma R. Olsen, comps., "Rugged Men of the West," *Chronicles of Courage*, vol. 6 (Salt Lake City: International Society Daughters of Utah Pioneers, 1995), 374.

8. Nymphus Coridon Hanks, *Men of the Rockies: People I Have Known in the Shadow of the Hills* (Heber City: 1944 no publisher), 32–33.

9. Malouf and Olsen, comps., "Rugged Men of the West," 375–76.

10. Edward W. Tullidge, *The History of Salt Lake City* (Salt Lake City: Edward Tullidge, 1886), 168.

11. Hanks and Hanks, *Scouting for the Mormons on the Great Frontier*, 191.

12. Malouf and Olsen, comps., "Rugged Men of the West," 376–77.

13. Solomon Farnham Kimball, *Thrilling Experiences* (Salt Lake City: Magazine Printing Co., 1909), 87.

14. Hanks and Hanks, *Scouting for the Mormons on the Great Frontier*, 78–80.

15. Richard Kay Hanks, "Eph Hanks, Pioneer Scout," Master's Thesis, Brigham Young University (copy on file at Salt Lake City: LDS Church History Library, 1973), 113.

16. Kimball, *Thrilling Experiences*, 97.

17. Malouf and Olsen, comps., "Rugged Men of the West," 379.

Edward Hunter

1793–1883

Edward Hunter, an early stalwart of the Church, served as a bishop for many years. After the Saints arrived in Utah, Edward was called as the Presiding Bishop of The Church of Jesus Christ of Latter-day Saints. He was a good friend of Brigham Young and as a wealthy businessman, provided much financial assistance to the Church.

Apostle Orson F. Whitney said that Edward Hunter was "honest, straightforward in his dealings, and candid even to bluntness in his speech, his heart overflowed with kindness and he enjoyed the love and confidence of all. Childlike and humble, he was nevertheless shrewd and discerning. He was charitable and open-handed to all. . . . He was not only quick to perceive, but ready and witty at retort. . . . He was a great exhorter to faithfulness, particularly in the payment of tithes and offerings. His familiar speech at the Bishop's meetings [was]: 'Pay your tithing and be blessed.' "[1]

Edward Hunter was born 22 June 1793, in Newton, Pennsylvania. When he was twenty-two years old, he was offered the position of Justice of the Peace but declined because of his youth. He was later elected County Commissioner for Delaware County. When Edward was offered a position in the Pennsylvania legislature, he would not accept because he was a Democrat and wanted to remain one. He married Ann Standly sometime around 1833.

In regards to religion, Edward stated, "I always had an inquiry of the Lord as to how I could worship Him acceptably. . . . I attended different places of worship . . . but could not connect myself with any."[2]

When a nearby schoolhouse burned down in 1833, Edward offered to build a new one for the town if the residents would allow everyone to meet in it to worship God, no matter what their faith. This was agreed to; however, when two Mormon missionaries, Elijah H. Davis and Lorenzo Barnes, attempted to use the building to teach the gospel, local residents objected. Edward asked the people why they didn't want the Mormons preaching there, but received no clearer answer than the Mormons were a terrible people and that it wouldn't do to let them preach in their town. Edward reminded the people of their agreement, declaring that the Mormons would have their rights or else he would take back the building.

The missionaries then set up a meeting, which Edward attended. While Elder Davis was speaking, a man in the congregation, Robert Johnson, interrupted the missionary and tried to address the audience.

Irritated at Mr. Johnson's rudeness, Edward declared, "He is a stranger and shall have justice shown him and be respected; we will hear him and then hear you speak." As Elder Davis continued his sermon, a friend informed Edward that some of the men in the congregation planned to attack the missionaries after the meeting. Edward said, "I resolved as I lived that Mr. Davis should be protected, if I had to meet the rabble on their own ground. I kept my eye on them and determined to stand by him at the risk of person and property."[3] After the meeting, Edward stayed close to the missionaries, and they were not harmed.

That night, Edward lay awake pondering on what the missionaries had said. He then prayed, asking God, "Are those Mormons thy servants?" His prayer was answered quickly. Edward said, "Instantly a light came in the room at the top of the door, so great that I could not endure it. I covered my head with the bed-clothes and turned over to the wall."[4]

Edward was baptized in 1840.

Edward went to visit Nauvoo and while there, decided to buy a farm and several lots. He met and spoke with Hyrum Smith several times and during one of their conversations, talk turned to deceased loved ones. Edward asked Hyrum about the children he had lost. He was especially concerned about the recent death of his little son, George.

" 'It is pretty strong doctrine,' said Hyrum, 'but I believe I will tell it. Your son will act as an angel to you; not your guardian angel but an auxiliary angel, to assist you in extreme trials.' The truth of this was manifested to Edward about a year and a half later, when, in an hour of deep depression, the little boy appeared to him in vision."[5]

After he moved to Nauvoo, Edward was elected to the City Council and was chosen to be a body guard for Joseph Smith. There were a number of times when he hid the Prophet in his home.

As a wealthy man, Edward was able to employ a great many people on his numerous farms and properties, which was a great boon to the impoverished Saints. He was also generous in his donations to the Church. When Edward moved to Nauvoo, he brought with him seven thousand dollars in cash and four or five thousand dollars in goods, all of which he gave to the Prophet Joseph Smith. He gave so much that Joseph "finally told him he had done enough, and to reserve the rest of his property for his own use."[6]

In 1843, Edward was arrested, along with a few other brethren, on charges of treason. He was taken to Carthage to wait until he was to stand trial, but was later set free. The following year, Joseph asked Edward Hunter and two other men, J. Bills and P. Lewis, to meet with Governor Ford and see what could be done to stop the persecution of the Saints. Unfortunately, they were unable to meet with the governor. Edward arrived back in Nauvoo the same day that Joseph and Hyrum were murdered. When the brother's bodies were brought back to Nauvoo, Edward and a few other men took Joseph's body to the Mansion House. That night, Edward helped carry Joseph's body to the Nauvoo House, where Joseph and Hyrum were buried.

After the martyrdom, the great question on everyone's mind was who would lead the Saints. On 8 August 1844, Edward went to a meeting near the temple to hear Sidney Rigdon and Brigham Young speak. Sidney mounted a wagon box so he could be seen and heard better and spoke for an hour and a half. After lunch, Brigham Young had his turn.

Edward said he was sitting, listening, with his head in his hands when he heard a familiar voice. He said it "was the Prophet's voice as natural and true" as he had ever heard it. Edward said he "raised up quickly, fully expecting to see the Prophet, and I did. There he stood and gradually changed to that of Brother Brigham, but the voice was not Brother Brigham's. It was still the Prophet's." Then, another heavenly manifestation occurred, which only a few other people saw. Edward said, "Beside Brother Brigham, I saw the Prophet, who turned toward the speaker and smiled."[7]

On 22 November 1844, Edward Hunter was ordained a high priest and set apart as a bishop by Brigham Young. Edward presided over the Fifth Ward of Nauvoo for two years. After the Saints left Nauvoo, Edward was called to be the bishop of the Seventh Ward at Winter Quarters.

Brigham Young appointed Edward as a captain over one hundred wagons. He left two months after Brigham took the first contingent across the plains and arrived in the Salt Lake Valley on 29 September 1847. Edward said of their arrival, "We were all well, but our teams were worn down. . . . Our breadstuffs were very limited and we used to get roots from the Indians and dig them ourselves."[8]

Before leaving Nauvoo, Edward had collected good seed corn, which he gave to the first group of pioneers to cross the plains so they could plant crops for the Saints that were to follow. He wrote to missionaries and urged them to bring back choice seeds and cuttings of fruit trees. After his arrival in the valley, Edward became president of the Deseret Agricultural and Manufacturing Society, a position he held from 1856 to 1862.[9]

When Edward had left for the valley, his second wife had decided to stay behind for a time. When Brigham returned to Winter Quarters, Edward sent money with him to give to Laura so that she could travel to the valley when she wanted. Anxious about her welfare, Edward wrote to Brigham, saying, "I will be much obliged if I could receive from your hand how Laura is getting on that I may prepare for her."[10] Brigham did as he was asked.

After his arrival in the Salt Lake Valley, Edward Hunter was appointed the bishop of South Fort. He became well-known as a wise, knowledge-able businessman and was, by profession, a farmer, a leather curer, and a cattle expert. Two years later, in February 1849, Edward was called to be the bishop of the 13th Ward in Salt Lake City. That fall, Brigham Young asked Edward to go back to the Missouri River and organize the emigra-tion of the poorer Saints who had not yet been able to make the trek to the Salt Lake Valley. Edward fulfilled this assignment and returned a year later, on 10 October 1850.

The office of Presiding Bishop was the last General Authority-level office to be put into place by Joseph Smith. When this office was first authorized by revelation in 1841, Newel K. Whitney and George Miller functioned jointly in that position and when George Miller left the Church,

Bishop Whitney acted alone. When Newel K. Whitney passed away, Edward Hunter was called to be the Presiding Bishop of the Church on 7 April 1851. He served for a year on a trial basis. Interestingly enough, his counselors, although they were never formally set apart, were Presidents Brigham Young and Heber C. Kimball.[11]

Later, Bishop Leonard W. Hardy and Bishop Jesse C. Little were designated as Edward's counselors. In an editorial printed in the Deseret Weekly News in 1851, the administrative relationship between Brigham Young and Edward Hunter was defined. "It is the duty of the Presiding Bishop to preside over all bishops, and clerks, and laborers in temporal affairs, and instruct, and counsel, and dictate as he shall be led by the Holy Ghost; and if he shall counsel wrong, it is the business of the First Presidency to correct him, and from whom he receives his instructions."[12]

It was a heavy charge for one man to be responsible for directing the work of all local bishops, overseeing all of the Church's temporal affairs, and making sure that all Aaronic Priesthood offices were filled and honored.

Brigham Young clarified the latter assignment when he told Edward that "it was the duty of the Presiding Bishop to have a full quorum of Priests, Teachers, and Deacons, properly organized in every stake of Zion, and hold their regular meetings."[13]

Additionally, the Presiding Bishop of the Church was to help furnish the means for immigration, colonization, public works, and domestic industry in Utah. Edward had to be aware of the economic and political movements in the territory, and as assistant trustee-in-trust, he probably knew more about the Church finances than anyone else. Although the general tithing office contributed funds, it was Bishop Hunter that kept track of the transportation of Church resources and the mobilization of those resources.[14]

To meet these weighty responsibilities, Edward met twice a month with local bishops and other leaders in Salt Lake City to coordinate efforts regarding public works, tithes, resources, immigration, and the needy.[15]

In 1877, Bishop Hunter sent out a letter that instructed bishops on a variety of matters, such as: "tithing, meetings ('let them be short and spiritual'), fast offerings, testimony meetings ('have no preaching sermons') selecting block teachers ('select the best and wisest men') and solving disputes ('have all grievances and disputes settled by the lesser priesthood.')"[16] He also told local bishops that they were responsible for the welfare of the Indians.

Tithing was one of Bishop Hunter's foremost responsibilities. He oversaw tithing operations at the general tithing storehouse in Salt Lake City and also in wards throughout the Church. Because the Church was so poor and had to rely heavily on voluntary donations for financial support, Edward took particular pains to encourage the Saints to pay their tithing. By careful administration of incoming funds, Edward was able to help provide the Church with the necessary economic foundation to grow and carry out its spiritual functions.

When he became Presiding Bishop, Edward Hunter did not inherit any smoothly-working tithing operation. Instead, he had to create, refine, and manage a complicated non-cash tithing system that would pump economic life into the Church. Edward was responsible for receiving, storing, allocating, and accounting for animal and produce tithes, as well as property and labor tithes, and some cash tithing. This was an exceptionally complicated process, since the majority of the Saints paid their tithes in kind or with personal labor. It was difficult to fix prices for specific items such as a bushel of new oats, two hours labor for mending a fence, or the price of a three-year-old sheep.

As a businessman, Edward was able to counsel local bishops on what items they should trade and which they should sell, as well as how much each item was worth. To help handle tithing, Edward used "agents to help funnel the tithes, [such as] traveling bishops, regional presiding bishops who managed regional tithing stores, and various traveling agents."[17]

It took a wise man to collect tithing and a wiser one to distribute it equitably. In order to balance supply and demand throughout hundreds of Mormon settlements, Edward Hunter carefully monitored the needs of the Saints, kept an eye on the weather, stayed informed of all incoming immigrants, and projected future crop harvests. "As manager of tithing products of all kinds, Bishop Hunter constantly aced four main problems: 1) Making proper valuation of goods; 2) Storing perishable goods; 3) Transferring goods around to meet the overall needs of the kingdom; and 4) Record keeping."[18]

As Presiding Bishop, Edward Hunter met regularly with President Young and other Church leaders. On 6 April 1853, he laid the southwest cornerstone of the Salt Lake Temple, and afterwards, he spoke to the congregation.[19]

All though the 1850s and 1860s, Bishop Edward Hunter was among President Young's inner circle of advisors and administrators. William G.

Hartley, of the LDS Church Historical Department, remarked, "Edward Hunter earned a reputation as a great man because he learned how to be a good number two man to the strong-willed Brigham Young. His firm hand on the Church's temporal reins helped steer it through dramatic transformation in size and procedures."[20]

Besides depending upon Edward to collect and manage the tithes of the Church, Brigham Young also relied on him to have local bishops supply men from their wards to work as stonecutters for the temples, provide labor for building roads, and for various other jobs. "Bishop Hunter was always there to take care of things, and President Young knew that he would be, always performing the job that needed to be done."[21]

While Brigham Young had often chastised Bishop Hunter's predecessor, Newell K. Whitney, Edward was never reprimanded. President Young commented on this, saying of Edward, "I knew he came into this Church and had transacted business on a large scale, was a good and competent judge of horses, cattle, cows, grain, etc.; and therefore did not need those severe chastisements that some of you bishops are obliged to take from time to time."[22]

Edward Hunter was also a key officer of the Perpetual Emigrating Fund Company. As such, he directed the welfare program on behalf of the immigrants and was often called upon to assist the needy.

Part of Edward's responsibilities included finding work for new emigrants after companies arrived in the Salt Lake Valley. As an well-organized leader, Brigham Young had an effective system in place to take care of the newcomers. A visitor from the eastern states, who was invited to see firsthand how this process operated, related the following:

> Last Sunday . . . Brigham Young sent for us . . . to see a private meeting of the bishops and to hear what kind of work these reverend fathers had met to do. . . . Edward Hunter, their presiding bishop, questioned each (local bishop) . . . as to the work going on in his ward, the building, painting, draining, gardening; also as to what this man needed, and that man needed in the way of help. An emigrant train had just come in, and the bishops had to put six hundred persons in the way of growing their cabbages and building their homes. One bishop said he could take five bricklayers, another two carpenters, a third a tin man, a fourth, seven or eight farm servants, and so on through the whole bench. In a few minutes I saw that two hundred of these poor emigrants had been placed in a way of earning their daily bread.[23]

In 1872, Brigham Young went to St. George for the winter. He was approaching his seventy-second birthday, which was beyond the normal life expectancy of that time, and found that the warmer climate of St. George helped ease his rheumatism pains. Away from the crushing pressures that were constantly upon him in Salt Lake City, Brigham was in good spirits when he wrote Bishop Edward Hunter on 11 January 1873. "My health is much improved since I left your city. I am having a good rest, both mentally and physically, in this mild climate. . . . The brethren are sowing grain, pruning vineyards, working in their gardens, etc., while the birds are singing as though it were May."[24]

President Young passed away in 1877, but Edward Hunter continued to serve faithfully. In his later years, Edward said, "I have acted in the Priesthood and the part allotted me, with the love and fear of God before my eyes, by the aid of His Spirit to the best of my ability, and I hope acceptably in the sight of God and those who preside over me in this Latter-day work."[25]

Edward Hunter was ninety years old when he died in Salt Lake City on 16 October 1883. He had served faithfully for sixty-two years, carrying out every duty assigned to him. Orson Whitney wrote, "So passed from this stage of action, where for over ninety years he had acted well and faithfully every part assigned him, a man of God as noted for his uprightness and integrity, as for his genial nature and overflowing kindness of heart. His memory will live as long as the great work with which he was identified, and which he labored so long and faithfully to establish."[26]

Notes

1. Andrew Jenson, *Latter-day Saint Biographical Encyclopedia*, vol. 1, 4 volumes, (Salt Lake City: Andrew Jenson History Company, 1901), 232.

2. Ibid., 228.

3. Ibid., 229.

4. Ibid.

5. Ibid., 229–30.

6. Ibid., 230.

7. Francis M. Gibbons, *Brigham Young, Modern Moses/Prophet of God*, (Salt Lake City: Deseret Book, 1981), 104.

8. Jenson, *Latter-day Saint Biographical Encyclopedia*, vol. 1, 231.

9. William E. Hunter, ed. by Janath Russell Cannon, *Edward Hunter,*

Faithful Steward, (Salt Lake City: Mrs. William E. Hunter, 1970), 274.

10. Ibid., 222.

11. William G. Hartley, "Edward Hunter: Pioneer Presiding Bishop," in Donald Q. Cannon and David Whittaker, eds., *Supporting Saints* (Salt Lake City: Bookcraft, 1985), 278.

12. Donald Gene Pace, "The LDS Presiding Bishopric, 1851–1888: An Administrative Study," Master's thesis, Brigham Young University (copy on file at Salt Lake City, LDS Church History Library, 1978), 113.

13. Hartley, "Edward Hunter: Pioneer Presiding Bishop," 295.

14. Hunter and Cannon, *Edward Hunter, Faithful Steward*, 275, 279.

15. Larene Porter Gaunt, "Edward Hunter, Generous Pioneer, Presiding Bishop," *Ensign*, Jul. 2004, 51.

16. "A Pioneering Bishop," Church Section, *Deseret News*, Jun. 20, 1981, 12.

17. Hartley, "Edward Hunter: Pioneer Presiding Bishop," 288.

18. Ibid., 286.

19. Hunter and Cannon, *Edward Hunter, Faithful Steward*, 136, 143.

20. William G. Hartley, "Edward Hunter: Pioneer Presiding Bishop," 286.

21. Ronald G. Watt, "Edward Hunter," Church Section, *Deseret News*, Apr. 24, 1976, 16.

22. "A Pioneering Bishop," Church Section, *Deseret News*, Jun. 20, 1981, 12.

23. Robert B. Day, *They Made Mormon History* (Salt Lake City: Deseret Book, 1973), 45.

24. Gibbons, *Brigham Young, Modern Moses/Prophet of God*, 255–56.

25. Jenson, *Latter-day Saint Biographical Encyclopedia*, vol. 1, 231–32.

26. Ibid., 232.

Daniel W. Jones

1830–1915

Daniel W. Jones, a celebrated scout, tireless settler, and stalwart missionary to the Indians, was one of those who went to the rescue of the handcart pioneers in 1856. During October's General Conference, President Young informed the Saints that two handcart companies had been caught in early snowstorms and needed help. In his no-nonsense manner, Brigham told the people that he wanted twenty teams ready by morning, and if they weren't voluntarily furnished, he would call upon the marshal to furnish them from teams left on the street.

Daniel left quickly, but the weather soon turned cold and stormy. He and his companions ran into a blizzard at Green River, and they were forced to take shelter for a time. When they finally reached the Willie Handcart Company, Daniel said, "A condition of distress, here met my eyes that I never saw before or since. The train was strung out for three or four miles. There were old men pulling and tugging their carts, sometimes loaded with a sick wife or children—women pulling along sick husbands—little children six to eight years old struggling through the mud and snow."[1]

In another account, Daniel reminisced, "On arriving we found them in a condition that would stir the feelings of the hardest heart.... They were out of provisions and really freezing and starving to death."[2]

He continued, "As night came on the mud would freeze on their clothes and feet ... There were hundreds needing help. What could we do? We ... helped as many as we could.... This was a bitter, cold night and we had no fuel except very small sage brush. Several died that night."[3]

In another account, Daniel wrote, "The morning after our arrival nine were buried in one grave ... I remember hearing Charles Decker remark that he had crossed the plains over fifty times [carrying mail] and this was the darkest hour he had ever seen."[4]

Later, Daniel Jones, Joseph A. Young, and Abe Garr, rode on to reach the Martin handcart company. Sister Scott was one of the first in that company to see the rescuers. She jumped to her feet, screaming, "I see them coming! I see them coming! Surely they are angels from heaven!"[5]

Daniel had planned on assisting the handcart pioneers to Salt Lake City. However, circumstances would dictate that Daniel and twenty other men would spend that long, cold winter in the wilderness, where they very nearly starved to death.

Daniel's allegiance to The Church of Jesus Christ of Latter-day Saints was a far cry from his earlier days when he had been convinced that all Mormons were evil and wicked. Daniel was born in Booneslick, Missouri, in August of 1830. When he was nineteen, he joined the Missouri Volunteers under Colonel Alexander Doniphan and marched from Santa Fe, New Mexico, to California in 1849. After Daniel was released, he was traveling through Utah in August of 1850, when he was accidentally shot.

Thomas, one of Daniel's closest friends, told Daniel that his wound needed treatment and that he ought to go to the closest settlement to get help. However, when Daniel learned it was a Mormon town, he refused to go, saying the Mormons were a bad people, and that they had been driven out from living among decent folk because they were thieves and murderers. Astonished, Thomas told him that not one word of that was true. When Daniel replied that he only knew what he had been told, Thomas said, "Then wait and see for yourself; they are the best people you ever saw."[6]

Although Daniel would not allow his companions to take him to the Mormon settlement at Spanish Fork, he agreed to let them set up camp nearby. When the Saints came to trade and visit, Daniel was wary of them, but said, "I could see nothing that indicated depravity, but on the contrary, all seemed industrious, kind, honest, and peaceable, ever ready to do us a favor or give any wanted information frankly, without any show of craftiness whatever."[7]

Daniel finally relented and allowed his friends to take him to the Mormon settlement. There, the Saints nursed him and took care of him. Because of their kindness, Daniel decided to stay and find out more about Mormonism. Daniel went to Manti during the winter of 1851, and boarded with Isaac Morley, who taught him about the gospel. Daniel gained a testimony that the gospel was true and asked to be baptized. On the day of his baptism, it was so cold that Isaac Morley had to use an ax to cut the ice so Daniel could be immersed.

On 29 January 1852, Daniel married Harriet Emily Colton, and they made their home on a farm near an Indian village. Daniel had always been concerned about the well-being of the Indians, and when he became acquainted with Brigham Young, he found that the Prophet shared his concern.

Knowing that Daniel had great influence with the Indians, President Young asked if he could do anything to stop the slave trade between the Indians and the Mexicans. Daniel replied that he would try, but that first, the Mexicans had to stop pressuring the Indians to sell their children. Brigham made arrangements to meet with a group of traders from Mexico and asked Daniel to go with him and act as his interpreter. In the spring of 1853, Daniel again went with President Young to act as an interpreter when the Prophet tried to stop the slave trade.

A few years later, Daniel went to the rescue of the handcart pioneers. Daniel and the men did all they could to help the stricken Saints. In order to move the suffering pioneers more quickly to Salt Lake City, it was suggested that their imperishable goods be left there with someone to watch them over the winter. When this idea was proposed to Captain Grant, he said, "I have thought of this, but there are no provisions to leave and it would be asking too much of anyone to stay here and starve for the sake of these goods; besides, where is there a man who would stay if called upon?"

Daniel was quick to answer, saying, "Any of us would."[8]

After much discussion, Captain Grant asked twenty men to stay and guard the goods. Daniel W. Jones and two other men were from the Salt Lake Valley, and seventeen men were from the emigrant trains. Daniel remarked, "There was not money enough on earth to have hired me to stay. I had left home for only a few days and was not prepared to remain so long away; but I remembered my assertion that any of us would stay if called upon. I could not back out."⁹

For the handcart pioneers to leave their belongings was no light matter. The two hundred wagons contained everything they possessed, and for the handcart pioneers to leave all their earthly possessions was to abandon everything they had on earth. They were only allowed to keep one set of clothes, some bedding, and a few light cooking utensils.

Since it was October and snow was already deep, there was no hope that supplies from Salt Lake City could be sent until May. The men thought they could depend on hunting to supply them with food, but game soon became scarce and the little bit of flour the men had was quickly gone. Soon, the only food they had was poor meat scrounged from cattle that had died near the fort, and they had to fight with the wolves to get that.

Near the end of December, Ephraim Hanks and Feramorz Little rode to a nearby fort. They were encouraged to find a letter from President Young, who advised them to be careful since they were in Indian country. Brigham urged them: "[Be] faithful and watchful, living your religion . . . do not go from your fort in small parties of one, two or three at a time . . . go in bands of some ten or twelve together and let them be well armed . . . try to ration out your flour as to have it last until we can send you relief . . . which may not reach you until May."¹⁰

After reading this letter, Daniel said, "It was plain to see that Brother Brigham was not apprised of our condition. He (Brigham) afterwards said if he had known our situation he would have relieved us if it had taken half the men in the valley."¹¹

Completely out of food, Daniel said, "Things looked dark, for nothing remained but the poor raw hides taken from starved cattle. We asked the Lord to direct us what to do. The brethren did not murmur, but felt to trust in God. We had cooked the hide, after soaking and scraping the hair off until it was soft, and then ate it, glue and all. This made it rather inclined to stay with us longer than we desired.

"Finally I was impressed how to fix the stuff and gave the company advice, telling them how to cook it; for them to scorch and scrape the hair off; this had a tendency to kill and purify the bad taste that scalding gave it. After scraping, boil one hour in plenty of water, throwing the water away which had extracted all the glue, then wash and scrape the hide thoroughly, washing in cold water, then boil to a jelly and let it get cold and then eat with a little sugar sprinkled on it. . . . we asked the Lord to bless our stomachs and adapt them to this food."[12]

After seven long months, relief finally arrived in the spring. Although he had received several letters from Brigham at the fort, Daniel had expected a letter instructing him how to go about listing the thousands of items belonging to the handcart pioneers so they would go to their rightful owner. Having no instructions, Daniel prayed to know how to go about this overwhelming task. After the wagons were loaded, everyone started for home.

Brigham was very glad to see Daniel and when told the full story of the suffering the men had endured over the difficult winter, expressed his deepest sympathies. President Young then asked Daniel if he had been able to list the goods properly. Daniel replied that he hoped so but was not sure.

Brigham said, "Well, you acted according to my instructions, did you not?"

Daniel answered, "I did not get any instructions, and it was pretty hard on me." He then handed Brigham a book. "Here is a report of what we did; I hope it is satisfactory." After reading the report, Brigham told Daniel he had done everything exactly right. Later, the letter Brigham had asked to be sent to Daniel, explaining how to list the goods, was found on a clerk's desk, unsent. When Daniel read it, he said, "My report agreed with the whole of it. This confirmed me more than ever in my faith in inspiration."[13]

Despite careful record keeping, there were mix-ups, and some people did not receive all of their goods. When they accused Daniel of stealing from them, President Young was outraged. He fired off a letter to all the bishops in Utah, telling them to read it to the Saints.

The letter read in part: "We feel desirous to express ourselves perfectly satisfied with his [Daniel's] labors while there, and with the care that he has taken of the property intrusted to him. He has our confidence. And we say, God bless him for what he has done. The men who find fault with the labors of Brother Jones the past winter, we wish their names sent to this office, and when the Lord presents an opportunity, we will try them and see if they will do any better."[14]

With this assignment completed, Daniel went back to working as a trader, then returned to Salt Lake City in July 1857, after finding out that Johnston's Army was on its way to Utah. When he arrived in Salt Lake City, Brigham regretfully told Daniel that a formal complaint had been made against him, accusing Daniel of robbing the handcart pioneers. When Brigham asked Daniel if he would be willing to meet his accusers and answer their charges, Daniel stated that he would be glad to have that opportunity. Brigham then began talking about how he planned to deal with Johnston's Army, saying "the boys were going out to meet the army and see about getting the road clear . . . so they could see what was best to do."[15]

A few weeks later, on 25 August 1857, Daniel went to Brigham Young's office to meet with his accusers. Daniel explained how he and the others had nearly starved to death in order to watch over the pioneer's goods. After listening to the full story, Brigham asked if any of the accusers had anything to say. They did not. He asked if they thought Daniel was telling the truth. All answered yes.

Brigham then addressed them sternly: "You have accused Brother Jones of stealing from you and others. . . . These accusations commenced in the winter when Brother Jones and companions were eating rawhide and poor meat, suffering every privation possible to take care of your stuff. How such stories started when there was no communication can only be accounted for by the known power of Satan to deceive and lie."[16]

Brigham then started to pronounce a curse upon those who had accused Daniel, but Daniel stopped him, saying he could bear their accusations better than they could bear Brigham's curse. Afterwards, Brigham told Daniel that if he had set fire to the whole outfit and run off that winter, Brigham would not have blamed him.

With this matter resolved, Brigham asked Daniel, who was in the militia, to assist in his plans to protect the Saints. One of the tactics Brigham had decided upon was to have men hinder Johnston's Army as much as possible, so as to slow them down and allow time for a mediator, Thomas L. Kane, to reach a peaceful solution.

Daniel and other frontiersmen did their best. Speaking of the militia and the Mormon Raiders, Daniel said, "The boys on the plains made it very disagreeable for the advancing army nightly, running off their beef herd, burning their provision trains and the grass, and in every way possible impeding their progress. Finally, winter set in with severity, catching them in the mountains at Fort Bridger, where they were obliged to stay for the winter."[17] The following spring, the crisis was resolved peacefully and the Utah War ended.

In the spring of 1860, Daniel was asked by the United States Army to guide some troops to Santa Fe. Brigham felt this job was too danger-ous, because many Mexicans were still angry at the Mormons for stopping their slave trade. Brigham then sent George W. Bean to give Daniel the following message: "Tell Brother Jones I considered him one of my good boys and I do not want him to go off into that dangerous country and risk his life."[18]

Because of Brigham's advice, Daniel told the United States officer that he would only take the troops as far as Green River. However, when they arrived at Green River, the guide who was supposed to take over did not show up and Daniel was forced to continue. He guided the soldiers safely to Santa Fe, but on their way back, they were attacked by robbers.

Daniel moved to Provo for a time, then returned to Salt Lake City two years later. When problems arose between the Indians and settlers at the Uintah and White River Agency in the summer of 1871, Daniel said, "I made up my mind to act as a friend to the Indians in trying to get something done to better their condition." He then began working to pro-mote peace and understanding, doing his best to let the Indians know that the Mormons were their friends and telling them that Brigham was sorry when any of his people wanted to fight them.[19]

Not only did Daniel assist the Indians in dealing with the settlers, he also helped them cope with dishonest government Indian agents. These corrupt agents cheated the Indians and made them distrustful of whites. In an effort to recompense the Indians for what they had lost through the dishonesty of unscrupulous agents, Daniel went into debt. However, when Brigham found out what Daniel had done, he saw that Daniel was reim-bursed. Daniel said, "I acted as a trader most of the time, but my main busi-ness was to establish peace. It cost considerable time and money, and when I got through there was a debt of some $1,200.00 against me at Z.C.M.I. Brother Brigham ordered the account sent to him for settlement."[20]

Brigham then asked Daniel to help colonize a settlement in Sanpete County. Daniel wrote, "According to the request made by President Young I bought a lot and had a good, comfortable house built in Fairview, Sanpete County, expecting to make that my future home.... I was called upon by Henry Brizzee, about June, 1874, who told me that President Young wished to see him and me at his office to talk with us about a mission to Mexico."[21]

In this meeting, Brigham told Daniel and Henry that the time had come to prepare to introduce the gospel into Mexico. He advised Daniel and Henry to get their affairs in order, study Spanish, prepare themselves to translate portions of the Book of Mormon, and when they were ready, to report back to him.

Around this time, Daniel met Mileton G. Trejo, a Spaniard. Trejo had had a dream that prompted him to come to the United States and visit the Mormons. The dream had left such an indelible impression upon him that Mileton had come to Salt Lake City without even knowing enough English to even ask for a drink of water. Thinking Mileton might be able to assist in translating the Book of Mormon, Daniel invited the Spaniard to live with him. Daniel taught him the gospel, and eventually, Mileton was baptized.

Daniel met with President Young in 1875 to update him on developments. Brigham was pleased to hear about Mileton Trejo and the progress they had made in translating. He then asked Daniel to prepare sections of the Book of Mormon for printing, adding that the actual printing would have to wait, since Church funds were presently very low. When Daniel offered to raise the necessary funds, Brigham authorized him to collect enough to do the printing and to support himself and Mileton Trejo while they translated the Book of Mormon.[22]

Brigham then asked how Daniel was going to prove to Church leaders that his translation of the Book of Mormon was correct. Daniel proposed to have Church leaders select any book and Brother Trejo would translate it into Spanish. Then, without having seen the book, Daniel would translate it back into English. When Church leaders compared the final version with the original, they were completely satisfied that all was correct.[23]

In September 1875, Daniel left with fellow missionaries J. Z. Stewart, Heleman Pratt, Wiley C. Jones (Daniel's son), R. H. Smith, Ammon M. Tenney, and A. W. Ivins. Part of their mission included exploring Arizona on their way to Mexico. President Young hoped they could find water, as a large group of settlers that had recently been sent to colonize Arizona had just returned because they had run out of water and been unable to locate any. The settlers had thought they were going to die, but after praying, enough rain had fallen to allow them to fill their water barrels. They returned to Salt Lake City, and said Arizona was uninhabitable. After telling the story, Brigham asked Daniel, "What do you think of that, Brother Jones?"

Daniel replied, "I would have filled up, (the water barrels) went on, and prayed again."

Putting his hand on Daniel's shoulder, Brother Brigham avowed, "This is the man that shall take charge of the next trip to Arizona."[24]

The missionaries crossed the desert, and at Tucson, found a letter waiting for them from Brigham Young, giving them news and offering encouragement. They reached the border in January 1876 and became the first Mormon missionaries to enter Mexico.

In the first town the missionaries entered, the local padre gave a sermon detailing how evil the Mormons were, and asked people to shun them. The padre's sermon effectively stopped the elders from preaching, because the law required preachers to speak in a special house and now, no one in the village would allow them access to one. Then Daniel had an idea.

Before leaving Salt Lake City, President Young had given Daniel a new set of saddler's tools, saying enigmatically that they might help Daniel out sometime when nothing else would. Daniel and his son, Wiley, rented a house, a bench, and a vise. Using the saddler's tools, they were able to open a saddle shop. As people began stopping by, Daniel and Wiley were able to make friends.

Daniel said, "I wrote to President Young regularly. We received letters from him in return, giving us kind encouragement and instructions. I reported to him our finances, which were getting short, stating that we intended going on and working our way through the best we could. We received a postal card directing us to wait till we heard from him. When we did hear it was in the shape of postal orders for money sufficient to bear our expenses for some time."[25]

In one of his letters to Daniel, Brigham Young wrote, "Do not court opposition, but move steadily on, presenting the truths of the gospel to those who will hear you." Brigham ended his letter, "With love to yourself and all the brethren associated with you, and with constant prayers that you may enjoy all the blessings that in your heart you can righteously desire and that abundant success may crown your labors, I remain 'Your brother in the Gospel,' Brigham Young."[26]

When their mission was concluded, Daniel and his son, Wiley, started for home. They stopped in Kanab to see President Young, who was visiting there. Daniel said, "He was glad to see me and hear the report from Mexico."[27] Daniel and Wiley arrived home on 1 July 1876.

Daniel had only been home one month when President Young asked him to start a new colony in Arizona and to choose a few families to go with him. When Brigham remarked that he wanted this settlement to succeed, Daniel remarked, "Give me men with large families and small means, so that when we get there they will be too poor to come back, and we will have to stay." Brigham laughed and said that was a good idea.[28]

When Daniel heard that some of the settlers did not want him to be in charge, he asked President Young to appoint someone else. But Brigham told Daniel to remember that "an angel could not please everybody." Brigham added, "You know how to travel, how to take care of teams. You are better acquainted with the roads, the country, the natives and their language, and are better prepared to take charge of a company than any one I know of."[29]

In 1877, Daniel and ten other families started for Arizona. They stopped in Santa Clara and President Young, who was in southern Utah at the time, drove out to give them his blessing and a few words of advice. Daniel said, "This was the last time I ever saw Brother Brigham—to me the best and greatest man I have ever known."[30] President Young passed away later that year.

The group made their way to the Salt River in Arizona. Brigham counseled Daniel in one of his letters, saying, "Live so as to retain within you the Spirit of the Lord, that it may be to you a present helper in every time of need . . . be just one toward another, and kind and friendly with all men; do your utmost by precept and example to win the hearts of the Lamanites, and ever use the influence you acquire over them for good, for their salvation and education."[31]

Daniel did win the hearts of the Indians. However, this caused unforeseen problems, for when trouble arose between the settlers and Indians, Daniel usually sided with the Indians, causing ill feelings among the settlers. Eventually, the settlers became so disgruntled, all but three families left. Despite this, Daniel continued to protect the rights of the Indians, who trusted him implicitly. He said, "Many persons were jealous of my influence with the natives and wondered how I managed to obtain so much power over them. I simply acted as a friend, and the Indians knew this."[32]

In 1885, Daniel was called on yet another mission, this time returning to Mexico to preach the gospel. After his return, Daniel moved back to Fairview.

Daniel W. Jones died on 29 April 1915, in Mesa City, Arizona. As a close friend of Brigham Young, Daniel did his best to faithfully fulfill every assignment the Prophet gave him. During his lifetime, Daniel served devotedly as a scout, missionary, colonizer, and peacemaker among the Indians, playing an important role in establishing peace between settlers and the Indians. He was one of the first missionaries to go into Mexico and later became the first President of the Mexico Mission. Daniel helped build the kingdom by assisting Mileton Trejo translate the Book of Mormon and other Church pamphlets into Spanish.

Notes

1. LeRoy R. Hafen and Ann W. Hafen, *Handcarts To Zion, the story of a Unique Western Migration, 1856–1860* (Glendale: The Arthur H. Clark Company, 1976), 115.

2. Daniel W. Jones, *Forty Years Among The Indians* (Salt Lake City: Bookcraft, 1960), 62.

3. Hafen and Hafen, *Handcarts To Zion, the Story of a Unique Western Migration, 1856–1860*, 115.

4. Daniel W. Jones, *Forty Years Among The Indians*, 62.

5. Hafen and Hafen, *Handcarts To Zion, the Story of a Unique Western Migration, 1856–1860*, 114.

6. Daniel W. Jones, *Forty Years Among The Indians*, 30.

7. Ibid., 33.

8. Ibid., 65.

9. Ibid., 70.

10. Ibid., 76–77.

11. Ibid., 77–78.

12. Ibid., 79–80.

13. Ibid., 107–8.

14. Ibid., 110.

15. Ibid., 112–13.

16. Ibid., 116.

17. Ibid., 121.

18. Ibid., 130.

19. Ibid., 183.

20. Ibid., 202.

21. Ibid., 211.

22. Ibid., 216.

23. Ibid., 219.

24. Ibid., 222.

25. Ibid., 253.

26. Ibid., 247.

27. Ibid., 285–86.

28. Ibid., 287.

29. Ibid., 289.

30. Ibid., 291.

31. Ibid., 295.

32. Ibid., 311.

John D. Lee

1812–1877

From the earliest days of Brigham Young's presidency, John Doyle Lee worked as an intrepid builder of the kingdom. Although his name is forever linked with the Mountain Meadows Massacre, he had served the Church faithfully for many years prior to that tragic event. John had always been devoted to Brigham Young and had proven himself to be a good friend. "That the feeling was mutual is shown by the fact that Lee was at once put into important positions."[1]

John D. Lee was born 12 September 1812 at Kashaskia, Illinois. He stood about 5'7," had a florid complexion, auburn hair, and light blue eyes. John was skilled in the use of a gun and an ax and was always ready to undertake new ventures.

From 1845 to January 1846, John spent most of his time working in the Nauvoo temple. Sometimes he didn't have time to go home to sleep, so he would spend the night in a side room. On 13 January 1846, Brigham Young called John D. Lee to keep records of the sealings.[2]

In April 1846, John and a few other men were sent on a trading expedition for the Church. During the trip, he met Patrick Dorsey, who was suffering from a problem with his eyes. Patrick asked John to give him a blessing. Shortly after the blessing, his eyes were healed. Patrick was so overjoyed, he traded very generously with John, which helped the Saints immensely. John was so successful at trading that Brigham Young sent him out repeatedly to act as a purchasing agent.[3]

Then, in August 1846, Brigham Young had a different assignment for John. The Prophet told him, "I have a very dangerous but responsible mission for you to perform. I want you to follow up the Mormon Battalion and be at Santa Fe when they receive their payment. Can you go?"

Although travelers were often attacked by outlaws and Indians, and he would be carrying a great deal of money when he returned, John accepted the assignment. He replied, "I am willing to do whatever I can to further the cause."

Brigham was aware that John's families had little food and that one of his wives was sick and had a two-week-old baby. He told John, "Go, and God will protect you. I shall see that your families do not want. It is most important that we have what money we can get if we are to have food to survive this winter."[4]

In the spring of 1847, as Brigham prepared to lead a group west, he asked John to stay to farm and raise food for the Saints at a place that became known as "Summer Quarters."

The following year, when plans were laid to have more Saints cross the plains, John told Brigham that he didn't think he could go west because he lacked the means to travel.

President Young replied that if he had the means to help, he would, then added, "I know your circumstances and I know your desires. You have helped me and I hope that I may have means to help you and you shall prosper." Embracing Lee, Brigham continued; "Go and prosper and be ye blest."[5] A few days later, President Young was able to loan John the items he needed so he could travel to the Salt Lake Valley in his company.

"During the months-long journey, so full of uncertainty, hardship, nervous tension, and acute danger, Young frequently sought Lee's advice, sometimes made him his confidant, and often called upon him to undertake some difficult or unpleasant task."[6]

After his arrival in Utah, John D. Lee, along with other Mormon leaders, worked under Brigham's direction to build a city, plow land for farms, and develop irrigation systems. It wasn't long before Brigham Young began sending groups of Saints to colonize new settlements. John attended one meeting where Brigham called for volunteers to go south. At the end of the meeting, Brigham talked with John, saying, "John, when I talked about making the settlement in the south, I meant you. If we are to establish an iron industry there, we must have a solid base of farming to help support it. We need men like you to produce food for the miners and mill workers . . . The kingdom cannot grow without men like you."[7]

So it was that in the General Conference of October 1851, John D. Lee's name was on the list of those appointed to go to new settlements. George A. Smith proposed that John establish a settlement at the junction of the Rio Virgin.

Obediently, John D. Lee went into an inhospitable land. He then "converted the raw wilderness into profitable farms, developed large herds of cattle, sheep, and goats, experimented successfully with many new agricultural products, including silk and cotton, founded settlements, built fences, dug irrigation ditches, erected saw, grist, and sugar-cane mills, played the role of explorer, dealt sternly or kindly with the Indians as occasion required, established and operated a ferry across the isolated, silt-laden waters of the Colorado . . . and preached as he was given opportunity."[8]

On 17 March 1852, John wrote to Brigham, saying, "Brother Brigham Young, I am a thousand times obliged to you for sending me to Iron County, not that I wanted to be away from you . . . but that it has placed me in circumstances where of necessity I had to rub up my talent . . . I have waded through trouble and passed through dark and trying hours and through experiences I have learned patience."[9]

Brigham Young visited the area in 1854 and, while there, designated the spot he wanted the settlers to build a new fort. John then devoted himself to helping build the fort and raising crops. By early 1855, all the Saints in the area were living at the new fort, even though it was not quite finished.

The Mountain Meadows Massacre occurred a few years later. In order to understand this horrifying incident a little better, it is necessary to be aware of the events that preceded it. For many years, the Mormons had been viciously persecuted. Raging mobs had destroyed the Saints' homes, farms, and possessions. A number of Mormons were murdered, along with Joseph Smith, their beloved Prophet and leader, and his brother Hyrum. After moving from place to place to escape the relentless persecution, the Saints built up a beautiful city, but were cast out of Nauvoo, and forced once again to start over in a harsh environment in the wilderness.

Then, after having isolated themselves in Utah to escape ruthless per-secution, the Mormons discovered that the United States government was sending an army to subdue them. The Prophet Brigham Young responded to this crisis by telling the Saints to make preparations in case they were forced to defend themselves against the invading troops.

While it is not certain exactly what precipitated the Mountain Mead-ows Massacre, people in the area reported that the emigrant company used vulgar epithets when speaking of Mormon leaders, boasted of par-ticipating in the murder of Joseph and Hyrum Smith, poisoned local water springs, and promised that they would return and fight with the army to kill the Mormons.[10] Whether these charges were true or not is a matter of speculation. What is certain is that after the massacre, many facts were suppressed, falsified, and distorted.

To this day, historians disagree on many aspects regarding the Moun-tain Meadows Massacre. However, most experts agree on the following facts. In 1857, Porter Rockwell informed Brigham Young that President James Buchanan had sent an army to Utah to put down a supposed Mormon rebellion and install a new governor. Brigham Young then declared martial law and asked the Saints not to sell any goods to immigrants that were traveling through the area. President Young called all missionaries home and sought support from the Indians. Members of the Quorum of the Twelve Apostles were sent throughout Utah to preach and to prepare the Saints for the coming army. George A. Smith was sent to southern Utah where he charged the Saints to be ready to defend Zion.

That summer, a wagon train of immigrants led by Charles Fancher camped at Mountain Meadows in southern Utah. It was alleged that some of the emigrants told local Mormons that after they had reached their destination in California, they would return and join the United States army to fight the Mormons. When Indians attacked the emigrants, local Church leaders sent James H. Haslem to Salt Lake City to ask Brigham Young what they should do.[11]

Brigham sent an urgent message with James H. Haslem, telling the Saints to leave the emigrants alone and not to interfere with them but to let them go in peace. As James prepared to leave, Brigham told him, "Go with all speed, spare no horse flesh. The emigrants must not be meddled with, if it takes all Iron County to prevent it. They must go free and unmo-lested."[12]

However, before James H. Haslem could return to southern Utah, local Church leaders joined with the Indians and attacked the emigrants again, killing all of them except for eighteen young children. Afterwards, John D. Lee, who took part in the attack, rode to Salt Lake City and told Brigham that the Indians were solely to blame for the attack. Others also covered up the facts regarding the massacre. In June 1858, the new governor of Utah, Alfred Cumming, issued a proclamation that restored peace to the Utah territory.

That November, John D. Lee purchased property in southern Utah in a little town called Washington. He was an industrious worker, and when Patriarch Isaac Morley and his wife, Alnora, came to visit, Isaac exclaimed, "Why, Brother Lee, I am astonished at what you have done. You have houses and land, flocks and herds, wives and children. I marvel at what you have accomplished."[13]

In May 1861, Brigham traveled south and stopped to visit John. Brigham discussed the condition of the Saints in the area and praised John for his industry, which showed itself in his homes, farms, and corrals. Brigham, still unaware of the truth surrounding the tragedy, also lamented the death of the emigrants at Mountain Meadows massacre.[14]

It was only later that Brigham began to learn the terrible truth, which was that the Mormons had been full participants in the massacre. Evidence in the LDS Church Archives and in government reports suggest that Brigham accepted John D. Lee's initial account that the Indians were to blame and did not know of Mormon involvement until sometime in the 1860s.

The truth started to come out when Jacob Hamblin, who served as a scout and a missionary to the Indians in southern Utah, went to Salt Lake City in June 1858 and told Brigham he was sure Mormons had participated in the massacre. Brigham took Jacob's report seriously and replied that he would get a court of justice to "ferret this thing out."[15]

As Brigham learned more, he relieved Church leaders in the area of their callings. The investigation moved along slowly, and some government authorities began claiming that Brigham himself had ordered the massacre. Sometime in the 1860s, John D. Lee was released as a bishop.[16]

John remained in southern Utah, ranching and farming. Early in 1862, southern Utah was deluged with rain, that lasted for an unbelievable forty days. Destruction was everywhere. Homes were ruined, and four mills, a molasses mill, orchards, vineyards, and the rock fort were all destroyed. In one of John's homes, a partition wall on an upper level collapsed, killing two of John's children. It took four years of hard work before John was able to fully restore his farms and homes.[17]

When Brigham Young left Salt Lake City on 24 February 1870, to go to southern Utah, John D. Lee went to the little town of Beaver to see him. That September, Brigham went south again and had a visit with John who, by this time, had become somewhat ostracized from his family and friends for his part in the Mountain Meadows Massacre.

During this trip, Brigham decided to start a settlement at Kanab and called Levi Stewart to be the bishop. Knowing that one of the first needs was for a saw mill, Levi asked Brigham if John D. Lee could be assigned to move to the area and help him build a mill. John was an acknowledged expert on new machinery and the two had worked together before. Brigham Young asked John to leave his long-established farm at Harmony and set up a sawmill in partnership with Bishop Levi Stewart.[18]

Loyal as always to the Prophet, John agreed and immediately put up his prosperous farms and home in New Harmony for sale. Within three weeks, John was ready to leave. It took him ten days to travel approximately one hundred miles to Kanab, as the wagons were heavily loaded and the road was steep at times. After reaching Kanab, John traveled on nearly three days to reach lower Skutumpah, the place where he would start anew and build a new home.[19]

John D. Lee was working on the mill and had begun to build a home when he received word in November that he had been excommunicated for his part in the Mountain Meadows Massacre. Two other men were excommunicated at the same time.

John wrote in general terms about his assignment in Kanab and his excommunication: "My love for the Truth is above all other things and is first with me, and believe that President Young has suffered this to take place for a wise purpose and not for any malicious intent. My prayer is, may God bless him with light and with the intelligence of Heaven to comprehend the things of God."[20]

In December, John rode to St. George to see President Young and try to clear himself of charges. John told Brigham that he did not understand why he was being cut off from the Church now, instead of thirteen years ago when the incident had taken place. Brigham replied that they [Church leaders in Salt Lake City] had not learned the facts and particulars of the tragedy until lately.[21]

Despite this, John remained loyal to the Church and to Brigham

Young, even after finding out that Brigham had initiated the disciplinary action shortly after asking John to move to his lonely outpost near Kanab.

In Southern Utah, there were a few dissenting factions that had broken off from the Church. Among them were the Godbeites, who were led by William S. Godbe. They were highly critical of Brigham Young's policy of isolationism and wanted to become integrated into the national economy so as to bring more wealth to Utah. John went about preaching, urging people to stay true to the gospel and not be deceived by these dissenters.

Late in 1871, John was asked to move to a wild area along the Colorado River crossing. The Colorado River was a formidable barrier to cross. There were only a few fords in hundreds of miles and those fords were often dangerous, being affected by high water.[22]

Aware of the problems associated with crossing the Colorado, Brigham Young ordered a ferry to be built near John D. Lee's home, so the Saints and other travelers could cross the river safely. John and his family were happy about the new ferry, for it meant that other people would settle there and their outpost would not be so lonely. This site eventually became known as Lee's Ferry, because John fashioned a ferry boat with the help of Tommy Smith. It was ready for launching on January 11.[23]

A few months later, Major John Wesley Powell was on an exploring expedition when he met Lee, whom he described as "a genial, courteous, and generous host."[24]

Just before sunrise on 19 January 1872, John heard the whoops and yells of a band of fifteen Navajos. When he went out, they asked him to ferry them across the river. Although John was sick, suffering from a fever and ague, he got the ferry ready with the help of his sons.

He was about to launch the ferry when his two sons became frightened; so his wife, Rachel, volunteered to go with him. When John and Rachel arrived on the far side, the Indians loaded down the ferry with blankets, cloth, linseys, and other supplies. After John and Rachel ferried them over, they went back for the Indian's horses. They tried to get the horses to swim alongside the ferry but the animals panicked and in the melee, nearly floundered the boat.

It was decided to take six Indians back across. They would take the horses downriver to another crossing. By the time John and the others recrossed the river, it was dark. John was so exhausted when he finally reached shore that he staggered and would have fallen had not one of the Indians caught him in his arms. Another Indian threw a blanket over him for warmth, and all of them helped John home.[25]

John continued running the ferry through 1873–1874. Then, he began going on exploring and prospecting trips, making careful maps and sending them to Brigham Young. John received a message from Brigham Young and George A. Smith, saying that they were glad to hear that John was "still interested in the advancement of our Setlements." Brigham also wrote about the ferry and promised to send chains to secure the boat, which he did promptly.[26]

In addition to his work as a ferryman, John built a stone house, dug ditches and canals for irrigation, visited Hopi and Navajo Indian villages, explored the surrounding wilderness and went on a long prospecting expedition for a group who hired him as an interpreter and guide.[27]

A federal grand jury was held on 24 September 1874, at Beaver, Utah regarding the Mountain Meadows Massacre. John D. Lee and eight other men were indicted. John was visiting one of his families in Panguitch, Utah, when he was arrested for his part in the Mountain Meadows Massacre. Although other leaders appeared as culpable, John D. Lee was the only one tried for murder.

John was imprisoned in the territorial penitentiary from 10 November 1874 to 23 July 1875, waiting for his trial. Sheriff William Stokes, who had arrested John, stated, "He never gave any trouble to me or his guards. He never tried to escape."[28]

While he was in jail, federal officials offered John his freedom, as well as money, if he would implicate Mormons in the massacre at Mountain Meadows. John refused, saying he would not lie. On 16 October 1875, he wrote: "I chose to die like a man [rather] than to live [like] a villain."[29]

At the conclusion of the trial, there was a two to one vote in favor of acquittal and Lee was sent to prison to await a second trial. Then, in May of 1876, John was released on bail. Despite the opportunity he had to disappear into the isolated regions around Lee's Ferry, John did not run.

A second trial was held in September 1876. New witnesses were brought forward and John D. Lee was convicted of murder. John was allowed to choose the style of execution—hanging, shooting, or beheading. He chose to be shot.

Nearly twenty years after the murders, on 23 March 1877, John D. Lee was taken to the site of the Mountain Meadows Massacre. Just before his execution, he was allowed to deliver his last message.[30]

John said, "I trust in God. I have no fear. Death has no terror." When he was finished speaking, John shook hands with those around him, and took off his coat, hat, and muffler. He sat on the edge of his coffin, with his hands untied, as he had requested, while a blindfold was put on. John D. Lee was then executed by a firing squad.[31]

Notes

1. Juanita Brooks, *John Doyle Lee, Zealot, Pioneer Builder, Scapegoat* (Logan: Utah State University Press, 1992), 63.

2. Ibid., 72.

3. Ibid., 84.

4. Ibid., 95.

5. Robert G. Cleland and Juanita Brooks, eds., *A Mormon Chronicle: The Diaries of John D. Lee, 1848–1876*, vol. 1, two volumes (San Marino: The Huntington Library, reprint edition; 1955), 25.

6. Ibid., 3.

7. Brooks, *John Doyle Lee, Zealot, Pioneer Builder, Scapegoat*, 154.

8. Cleland and Brooks, eds., *A Mormon Chronicle: The Diaries of John D. Lee, 1848–1876*, 4.

9. Brooks, *John Doyle Lee, Zealot, Pioneer Builder, Scapegoat*, 173.

10. Ibid., 223.

11. Arnold K. Garr, Donald Q. Cannon, Richard O. Cowan, eds., *Encyclopedia of Latter-day Saint History* (Salt Lake City: Deseret Book, 2000), 799.

12. Leonard J. Arrington, *Brigham Young, American Moses* (Urbana: University of Illinois Press, 1986), 258–59.

13. Brooks, *John Doyle Lee, Zealot, Pioneer Builder, Scapegoat*, 254.

14. Ibid., 267.

15. Arrington, *Brigham Young, American Moses*, 279.

16. Ibid., 280.

17. Brooks, *John Doyle Lee, Zealot, Pioneer Builder, Scapegoat*, 269–73.

18. Cleland and Brooks, eds., *A Mormon Chronicle: The Diaries of John D. Lee, 1848–1876*, vol. 1, 9.

19. Brooks, *John Doyle Lee, Zealot, Pioneer Builder, Scapegoat*, 292.

20. Ibid., 294.

21. Ibid., 295.

22. Ibid., 302.

23. Ibid., 315.

24. Cleland and Brooks, eds., *A Mormon Chronicle: The Diaries of John D. Lee, 1848–1876*, vol. 1, 10.

25. Robert Glass Cleland and Juanita Brooks, eds., *A Mormon Chronicle: The Diaries of John D. Lee*, vol. 2, two volumes, (San Marino: Huntington Library, 1955), 181.

26. Brooks, *John Doyle Lee, Zealot, Pioneer Builder, Scapegoat*, 333.

27. Cleland and Brooks, eds., *A Mormon Chronicle: The Diaries of John D. Lee, 1848–1876*, vol. 1, 10–11.

28. Brooks, *John Doyle Lee, Zealot, Pioneer Builder, Scapegoat*, 337.

29. Cleland and Brooks, eds., *A Mormon Chronicle: The Diaries of John D. Lee, 1848–1876*, vol. 2, 378.

30. Cleland and Brooks, eds., *A Mormon Chronicle: The Diaries of John D. Lee, 1848–1876*, vol. 1, 13.

31. Brooks, *John Doyle Lee, Zealot, Pioneer Builder, Scapegoat*, 367.

Jesse C. Little

1815–1893

As the President of the Eastern States Mission, Jesse C. Little was the voice of the Church in Washington during the exodus of the Saints from Nauvoo. Under the direction of Brigham Young, Jesse sought aid from the federal government as the Saints began to leave Nauvoo. It was largely through Jesse's persistent efforts as a diplomat that a Mormon Battalion was called up, supplying the Saints with the necessary resources to fund their trek across the plains.

Jesse Carter Little was born 26 September 1815 in Belmont, Maine. He was converted to the Church in 1839, and the following year, married Eliza Greenwood French. He later practiced polygamy.

Prior to his involvement with the United States Government, Jesse worked with George Bryant Gardner to publish a new book of hymns. Although several hymnals were already in existence,[1] this particular hymnal was unique in that it contained music, with written notes on a staff, while most hymnals of that time printed the text only. *The Little and Gardner Hymnal: A Collection of Sacred Hymns for the Use of Latter-day Saints* was published in 1844. Apparently Jesse understood the ability of music to enrich worship services and uplift church members.[2]

However, Jesse Little is best known for his role in working with the federal government to raise a Mormon Battalion. The Saints were preparing to evacuate Nauvoo in 1846 when Brigham Young called Jesse C. Little as the President of the Eastern States Mission. Brigham explained that a good part of Jesse's duties would be to serve as the Church's emissary to the United States government.

While Jesse was in Washington, Brigham wrote frequently, directing Jesse on matters he wished to pursue, most of which had to do with seeking governmental assistance and receiving compensation for the losses they had suffered because of persecution.

Brigham Young had heard that the government was planning to build a series of blockhouses and forts along the Oregon Trail. He thought the Saints could build them as cheaply as anyone and hoped to get a contract from the government to do this work as they traveled west.

Another idea Brigham had, was to win a contract from the government to freight provisions to Oregon and other points on the Pacific Coast. The money earned from either of these projects would enable the Saints to buy supplies for their westward trek. It would also pay for the migration of the poorer Saints, who otherwise would not be able to go.

Brigham told Jesse that if these ideas did not pan out, he should seek aid from the government in any practical form possible. Brigham said, "If our government shall offer any facilities for emigrating to the western coast, embrace those facilities if possible. As a wise and faithful man, take every honorable advantage of the times you can."[3]

While actively soliciting the government for aid, Brigham told Jesse to publicize how cruelly the Saints had been persecuted, in the hopes of arousing public sympathy for their plight, which could increase their chances of obtaining financial assistance. In addition, Brigham told Jesse to have Church members in the east prepare to travel west with the main body of the Saints to the place of refuge (which at this point had not been determined).

Jesse C. Little had gone to Philadelphia to preside over a Church conference when he met Thomas L. Kane, who would prove to be one of the best friends the Mormons ever had. Thomas had seen a notice in the newspaper about the conference and had attended out of curiosity. Afterwards, he introduced himself to Jesse.

Thomas was the son of Judge John W. Kane, a prominent lawyer, and had read about the plight of the Saints. A staunch advocate of the down-trodden, Thomas wanted to know more about the Mormons. He was sympathetic after Jesse told him about the many trials and hardships they had endured. The two men met several times during Jesse's stay in Philadelphia and became friends. When Thomas, a man of some influence, learned that Jesse was going to Washington to seek aid for the Saints, he gave Jesse a letter of introduction to Vice President George M. Dallas. This opened many doors that otherwise might have remained shut.

Jesse worked to obtain other letters of introduction. Governor John H. Steele of New Hampshire gave him a letter, vouching for Jesse's honesty and introducing him to George Bancroft, Secretary of the Navy. Jesse also got a letter of introduction from A. G. Benson, a local merchant, to Amos Kendall, former Postmaster General of the United States. Amos Kendall was a powerful man in Washington, and it was this introduction that eventually led to the arrangement of a private meeting between Jesse and President James K. Polk.

However, before Jesse arrived back in Washington, hostilities flared anew between the United States and Mexico. Trouble had been brewing with Mexico ever since Texas had secured its independence in 1836, but this latest conflict was so serious that President Polk declared war on May 13.

Jesse arrived in Washington on 21 May 1846. The next day, he attended a public reception where he was able to meet briefly with President Polk. Although he had very little personal time with the president, Jesse used the opportunity to ask for assistance for the Saints. Still, Jesse knew he would need an appointment with the president so they could have a meaningful discussion about obtaining assistance. He asked Amos Kendall for help in scheduling a private meeting. While he waited for this to be arranged, Jesse continued working with other government leaders to try and get a contract for the Saints to build forts on the Oregon Trail. However, it soon became clear that with the recent declaration of war, the president and other top officials were more concerned about getting soldiers than building forts.

When Jesse met with various officials to discuss how the government could help the Saints, talk turned to the idea of forming a battalion consisting of Mormon soldiers. When Jesse first presented this idea, Brigham was hesitant, but soon endorsed it as a means of defraying the cost of moving the Saints west.

With Brigham's approval, Jesse wrote a long, detailed letter to President Polk regarding the Mormon's plight and their recent expulsion from

Nauvoo. He explained that thousands of Mormons were determined to go west to escape persecution, but since they were poor and unable to pay their way, the enlistment of a Mormon Battalion could finance their journey. Jesse made it plain that the Mormons were ready and willing to provide troops to bolster the United States army.

Jesse's letter reached President Polk at a propitious time—just when he needed a large group of soldiers to leave quickly for the west. The United States had long felt that California was a desirable province, and they wanted to occupy the area before Europe and Mexico could get to it. President Polk decided it would be mutually advantageous, both to the Mormons and to the United States, to use Mormon manpower in these military operations. Raising a battalion of men from among the Mormons would help solve the United States pressing need for additional troops and also help the Saints who had been driven from their homes. After reading Jesse's letter, President Polk directed Amos Kendall to set up a meeting with Jesse.

On June 3, Jesse spent three hours with President Polk, using all of his persuasiveness to obtain help for the Saints. As a further bargaining tool, Jesse mentioned discreetly that the Saints might be forced to seek aid from another country if the United States government was unable to help them.

Jesse told the President that more than fifteen thousand people from Great Britain had joined the Mormon Church and of that number, almost five thousand had already emigrated to Mormon settlements in the United States and more were coming. This proved a strong negotiating point, since a people as numerous as the Mormons would pose a serious obstacle to the United State's westward expansion if the Saints joined either Mexico or Great Britain.

President Polk came to the conclusion that he could not ignore the Mormons. Yet neither did he dare give them too much aid. The President decided to send one thousand Mormon men by land and an equal number by sea to occupy the territory on the west coast. Although President Polk assured Jesse he was friendly toward Church members, his solution to raise a Mormon Battalion was mostly based upon a need for troops to leave immediately and the handy proximity of the Mormons who were— because of their situation—readily available.[4]

However, Thomas H. Benton, a congressman from Missouri, was violently opposed to President Polk's proposal. Benton tried to turn President

Polk against the Saints, claiming that the Mormons were disloyal to the United States. Benton came up with his own proposal, which was to send a Mormon Battalion to Mexico. The President liked the idea, as did Jesse.

Feeling encouraged by their discussions and wanting to reassure President Polk, who still doubted the loyalty of the Saints, Jesse C. Little wrote a letter to the president, declaring fervently: "If you will assist us in this crisis, I hereby pledge my honor, as the representative of this people, that the whole body will stand ready at your call, and act as one man in the land to which we are going; and should our territory be invaded, we will hold ourselves ready to enter the field of battle, and then, like our patriotic fathers, make the battlefield our grave or gain our liberty."[5]

Although President Polk reacted favorably to Jesse's letter, it was decided to change the original proposal. Instead of calling two thousand men, he called for a battalion of five hundred men to be mustered for twelve months.

Jesse left Washington on 9 June 1846, to discuss President Polk's offer with Brigham. Seeing this offer as a way of moving—at the government's expense—five hundred Mormon men to the West Coast, while providing money for the desperately poor Saints to buy supplies for their trek west, President Young authorized Jesse to accept the offer. Another important benefit of accepting this proposal was that the government would be much more likely to give the Saint's permission to camp on Indian lands over the winter. That was crucial, as it was too late in the year for the Saints to continue traveling and they did not have the necessary resources at that time for the long journey that lay ahead of them.

Jesse returned to Washington and began consulting with President Polk and his Secretary of War on how to go about having the United States Army recruit five hundred men to march to Santa Fe in support of General Stephen W. Kearny's military operations. Jesse negotiated to have the men given certain privileges with respect to discipline, payment structure, having their own officers, and so forth. The pay was approximately $21,000 for the entire group. Arrangements were made to pick up the battalion's pay at set intervals, so the money could be used to support the men's wives and children and to buy supplies for the Saints.[6]

When negotiations were finalized, Jesse C. Little and Thomas L. Kane went to St. Louis. From there, Jesse went to meet with Brigham Young and the general body of the Saints, while Thomas traveled to Fort Leavenworth, Kansas, carrying dispatches authorizing the mustering of a

Mormon Battalion. After receiving the dispatches, Captain James Allen, a recruiter for the United States Army, accompanied Thomas to Mount Pisgah. They arrived on 26 June 1846, with a commission to recruit five hundred Mormon volunteers to serve in the war with Mexico.

Although Brigham was pleased about the proposal to recruit a Mormon Battalion, many of the Saints were suspicious and wary. As a people, they had been deceived too many times to trust the government now. Some of the Saints felt that the Mormon Battalion was a thinly-veiled attempt to destroy or cripple the Mormons by taking their best men from them at a perilous time. While a few malicious politicians may have hoped for that, it was undoubtedly true that others, including President Polk, saw it as a way to aid the beleaguered Saints while helping the United States wrest California from Mexico.

Still, the Saints were hesitant and had to be persuaded by Brigham Young. It was fortunate that President Polk had lowered the number of men requested, as the Saints still felt that a battalion of five hundred men was far out of proportion to their numbers. It should be noted that the United States army never demanded that the Mormons form a battalion; they were only offered the opportunity to do so.[7]

Brigham Young became Captain Allen's chief aide in the recruitment, shuttling between Council Bluffs and Mount Pisgah to enlist men. Brigham encouraged the Mormon men to sign up, telling them that not only would they be aiding their country, they would also be blessing their people. Brigham explained that this recruitment would give the Saints much-needed cash and would provide an additional benefit in that the army would arm and equip the men at the government's cost. Finally, Brigham stressed that building up the Mormon Battalion would provide a way for the Saints to settle in a new home, free from persecution. He told the Saints, "We have lived near so many old settlers who would always say 'get out,' that we should be thankful for the privilege of going to settle a new country."[8]

Brigham had many plans for the funds the battalion would bring in. It was money that was desperately needed. Besides supporting the wives and children of the men who served in the Battalion, the money would be used to buy supplies such as sugar, shoes, wheat and other necessities. In a letter to Captain Jefferson Hunt and the other captains of the Mormon Battalion, Brigham wrote that "by the wisdom of heaven we will make every dollar sent us count as good as two or three at ordinary traffic."[9]

After the battalion had been mustered, Jesse accompanied the enlisted men as far as Fort Leavenworth. Brigham then asked Jesse to go west with him in the spring when the vanguard company of pioneers would head across the plains. Jesse returned east to resume his duties, while Brigham continued to move the Saints to Winter Quarters where they would wait out the winter.

On 26 February 1847, Brigham Young wrote to Jesse:

> I expect to start for the mountains before you arrive, as it is necessary for a pioneer company to be on the way as early as possible to insure crops ahead and I know of no better way than for me to go with the company, and if the brethren love me as I do them, they will not be long behind. I feel like a father with a great family of children around me, in a winter storm, and I am looking with calmness, confidence, and patience, for the clouds to break and the sun to shine, so that I can run out and plant and sow and gather in the corn and wheat.[10]

Early in the spring of 1847, Jesse left his wife and two children at Petersboro, New Hampshire and traveled three thousand miles to join Brigham Young. As predicted, Brigham had already left for the Salt Lake Valley, but Jesse caught up with him on 19 April 1847, when Brigham's company was about seventy miles west of Winter Quarters. Brigham Young then decided to organize the company into a military unit and appointed Jesse C. Little as adjutant.[11]

After Jesse arrived in the Salt Lake Valley, Brigham sent him, along with Samuel Brannan and Lieutenant W. W. Willis, to make preliminary explorations of Utah Valley. After twelve days of exploration, during which Jesse traveled approximately two hundred miles, he returned and gave President Young a favorable report. Brigham then asked Jesse to return east and resume his responsibilities there, presiding over the branches of the Church in New England and surrounding states.[12]

Five years later, in 1852, Jesse C. Little was released as mission president and moved his family to the Salt Lake Valley. Once he arrived, Jesse became prominent in ecclesiastical, civil, and military affairs, filling many important positions. To support himself, Jesse opened a hotel at Warm Springs in Salt Lake City. When an ordinance providing for the organization of a Fire Department in Salt Lake City was passed in October of 1856, Jesse C. Little was appointed chief engineer. He also served as a United States Marshal for Utah for a number of years. In 1856, Jesse was ordained to the office of a bishop and was set apart as second counselor to Bishop

Edward Hunter, serving faithfully for eighteen years. In 1874, he moved to Morgan County.

The Church lost a stalwart leader and a gifted ambassador when, after a long illness, Jesse C. Little died in Salt Lake City on 25 December 1893. Besides fulfilling his duties as President of the Eastern Mission, Jesse was instrumental in the enlistment of the Mormon Battalion, which helped the Saints when they were in desperate need of financial assistance from the United States government.

An obituary published in the Deseret News at the time of Jesse's death reported: "Colonel Jesse C. Little is dead, the Demise of One Who in the Prime of Life was Prominent Among the People. The announcement will bring into the minds of thousands in Utah, particularly the early settlers, memories of stirring events, whose importance has become more thoroughly understood through the lapse of time, in which Colonel Little was a prominent participator."[13]

Notes

1. Emma Smith had published a hymnal in 1835. *The Manchester Hymnal* was published in 1840 in England by Parley P. Pratt, Brigham Young, and John Taylor.

2. Marilyn J. Crandall, "The Little and Gardner Hymnal, 1844, A Study of its Origin and Contribution to the LDS Musical Canon," *BYU Studies*, vol. 44, #3, (2005), 137.

3. W. Ray Luce, "The Mormon Battalion: A Historical Accident?" *Utah Historical Quarterly*, Winter 1974, v. 42, 29.

4. Ibid., 32, 34.

5. *Chronicles of Courage*, vol. 5 (Salt Lake City: International Society Daughters of Utah Pioneers, 1994), 35.

6. *Journal History of the Church of Jesus Christ of Latter-day Saints*, 16 August, 1846 (Salt Lake City: LDS Church History Library).

7. Flora Belle Houston, *The Mormon Battalion* (Unpublished document on file in Salt Lake City: LDS Church History Library), 344.

8. Ibid.

9. Frank A. Golder, *The March of the Mormon Battalion, from Council Bluffs to California*, Taken from the Journal of Henry Standage (New York: The Century Co., 1928), 143–45.

10. Brigham Young, as quoted by Eugene England, *Brother Brigham* (Salt Lake City: Bookcraft, Inc., 1980), 154.

11. Andrew Jenson, *Latter-day Saint Biographical Encyclopedia*, vol. 1, four volumes (Andrew Jenson History Company: Salt Lake City), 243.

12. Milton R. Hunter, *Brigham Young the Colonizer* (Salt Lake City: The Deseret News Press, 1940), 34.

13. *Deseret Evening News*, 26 December 1893, 1.

Isaac Morley

1786–1865

Isaac Morley, leader of the small settlement of Manti, Utah, and his wife Hannah were given a dreadful ultimatum by the Indian chief, Joseph Walker—either give their baby to Chief Walker for one night, or the Indians would massacre everyone in the settlement.

It was 1850 and a few weeks earlier, some of the Indians decided they did not want to follow the rules set forth for the Mormon settlement. Tensions heightened and then threats were made, raising fear among the Saints. The situation deteriorated until Chief Joseph Walker, a proud and unpredictable leader, threatened to wage war upon the Saints in Manti.

He was thwarted in this by Chief Sowiette, an older chief who had led the tribe prior to Chief Walker. Chief Sowiette wanted peace and after an open confrontation between the two leaders, Chief Sowiette turned to his people and said, "Those who live in friendship with the Mormons, let them follow me."[1] Many Indians followed Chief Sowiette and walked away. When Chief Walker saw he did not have enough men to fight the settlers, he mounted his horse and rode off angrily.

Unfortunately, the matter was far from settled. When he returned,

Chief Walker went to Isaac Morley, saying he would make a peace treaty, but only on one condition—he wanted a token of trust. The token he asked for was a very specific one: the settlers were to give him a baby, which he would keep overnight. He didn't want just any baby; Chief Walker would only accept Simeon, the eighteen-month-old baby of Isaac and Hannah Morley. Chief Walker said he would return the baby the next morning. If Isaac should refuse, Chief Walker said he would destroy the entire settlement and kill all the people. He then left, saying he would return later for their answer.

Since it was well known that Chief Walker often sold stolen children to the Mexicans, Isaac and Hannah were in agony over this proposition. Ultimately, however, Isaac decided that it was better to lose their baby than the whole settlement and the child as well.

When Chief Walker returned, Isaac handed over his little son. The settlement joined together and prayed all night. When sunrise came, the anxious parents kept watching for the chief's return. Chief Walker kept his word and when he finally appeared, he was carrying little Simeon. This experience forged a special friendship between Isaac and Chief Walker.[2] Two weeks later, Chief Joseph Walker asked to be baptized. Father Morley baptized this famous Indian chief on 13 March 1850.[3] Three months later, Chief Walker was ordained an elder, the first of his tribe to be so honored.[4]

This incident was one of many ordeals that Isaac Morley experienced while he worked to build up Zion under the direction of Brigham Young.

Isaac Morley was born on 11 March 1786, at Montague, Massachusetts, and was a contemporary of both Joseph Smith and Brigham Young. He married Lucy Gunn in 1812, and later practiced plural marriage. At the time of his baptism, Isaac owned a large farm and a number of properties and after his conversion, he willingly donated them to the Church. Joseph Smith and his family lived with the Morley family during the Prophet's first winter in Kirtland. The Church of Jesus Christ of Latter-day Saints was organized in the Morley home, and later, Isaac built a frame home on his property for Joseph Smith to live in.[5] On 3 June 1831, Isaac was set apart as the first counselor to Edward Partridge, the first bishop of the Church. Later that month, in a revelation given to Joseph Smith, Isaac Morley was appointed to go on a mission to Missouri with Ezra Booth and preach the gospel (D&C 52:23).

In 1833, a mob demolished the printing office and house of W. W.

Phelps at Independence, Missouri, and tarred and feathered Bishop Edward Partridge. Fearing that the mob might harm others, Isaac Morley and five other men stepped up and offered themselves as a ransom, willing to be scourged or even killed to appease the mob of five hundred men who were armed with rifles, pistols, clubs, and whips.[6]

Along with other leaders, Isaac suffered many hardships and was once imprisoned for three weeks in Richmond, Missouri. In 1835, Isaac Morley served a mission in the eastern states.

After the Saints were expelled from Missouri, Isaac moved to Lima, where mobs burned down his house, cooper's shop, and destroyed all of his grain. When five of his neighbors were arrested on false charges of larceny, Isaac met with President Brigham Young, informing him that members of the mob had planted their own possessions on Mormon farms and then charged the Saints with stealing those items. Since it was highly unlikely that such a claim would be believed, Brigham advised Isaac to simply leave Lima and go to Nauvoo, which he did.[7]

Persecution followed the Saints, and when it became clear there was no alternative other than death, Brigham Young and other leaders decided to leave Nauvoo. Parts of the temple were dedicated so that temple work could be done, and Isaac and his wife were able to do their own work before fleeing the city. Brigham Young wrote, "I officiated in the [temple] with the brethren of the Twelve [Apostles]. We administered the ordinance of endowment to Isaac Morley and his wife Lucy."[8]

At Winter Quarters, Lucy contracted typhoid fever and died in January 1847. On 7 April 1847, Brigham asked Isaac to scout out arable land nearby where crops could be raised. Isaac and his group left with eight wagons, moving along the Ponca Road until he located suitable ground for raising crops. The site later became known as Kanesville and Brigham put Isaac Morley in charge of this area, which became known as "Summer Quarters."[9]

In the spring of 1847, President Young started west with a large company of pioneers, while Isaac stayed behind to direct the affairs at Summer Quarters. He saw that cattle were fattened for Saints who would leave in later companies, and kept in close touch with the people at Winter Quarters, while presiding over the High Council and visiting the wards at Summer Quarters and Winters Quarters. Many Saints went to him to receive counsel and blessings.

Later that year, President Young returned to Winter Quarters. The following spring, on 1 May 1848, Isaac Morley and a mammoth group of Saints left for Salt Lake City. "Isaac Morley was sustained as president of the caravan camp organization and Reynolds Cahoon and John Young were named as his counselors." Isaac's company consisted of 1,229 people, 397 wagons, and many horses, cattle, oxen, sheep, chickens, and other livestock.[10]

In mid-July, Isaac made a motion that the companies be divided into smaller ones to lessen the dust for the travelers, and so that the chore of pulling the wagons would be easier. This motion was passed by President Young. Isaac's wagon was among the first to enter the valley after a journey of 130 days. Isaac then settled his family in Sessions Settlement, a few miles north of the temple block.

During the first years in the valley, the Saints faced near starvation. To cut down on the loss of crops and animals from predators (over $1,000 worth of grain and stock had been destroyed by the animals), Brigham Young held a huge hunting contest. Isaac Morley and Reynolds Cahoon were chosen as judges, and when the contest was concluded, Isaac proudly met with Brigham Young to report on the large number of pests killed, which included wolves, foxes, magpies, and crows.[11]

The First Presidency took major steps in 1849 to "regularize church government" in the Salt Lake Valley. As part of this process, Isaac Morley, who was the oldest member of the High Council, was sustained as its president on February 12. Three days later, he was set apart by Brigham Young.[12]

In March 1849, the first election for the provisional government of the Territory of Deseret was held. Brigham Young was elected as governor, and Isaac Morley was elected a Senator in the Territorial Legislature.

Because the Saints had no temple where they could perform sacred ordinances, the tops of certain mountains were designated for this sacred work. On 21 July 1849, Isaac Morley went to the top of Ensign Peak with Brigham Young and a few other brethren to help officiate in sacred temple work so people could receive their endowments.[13]

In 1849, Isaac Morley participated in the first ever July 24th parade, which commemorated the entrance of the pioneers into the Salt Lake Valley. Isaac, a lieutenant in a company made up of men over fifty, rode in the parade with his group, which was called the "Silver Greys." A newspaper reported that during the parade, "Twenty-four Silver Greys led by Isaac Morley, patriarch, each having a staff painted red at the upper part and a bunch of white ribbon fastened at the top. One of them carried the stars and stripes bearing the inscription, 'Liberty and Truth.' "[14]

One of Brigham Young's goals was to have peace with the Indians. On 14 June 1849, Brigham met with Chief Joseph Walker to negotiate a peace treaty with the Ute Indian tribe. When Chief Walker told Brigham that he wanted to have the Mormons come and settle near him in the Sanpete Valley, Brigham sent out a group of settlers within six months. He asked Isaac, or Father Morley as he was often called, to preside over the new settlement.[15]

Part of the reason Brigham asked Father Morley to take charge of this important new settlement was because Isaac had proven himself to be a great organizer and leader during the trek west. So, on 28 October 1849, Father Morley—who was now sixty-four years old—left Salt Lake City with a group of thirty families. As he traveled along, more people joined the group until his company consisted of approximately 225 people. Continuing south, they reached the Sanpete Valley, which was approximately 100 miles south of Salt Lake City, on 22 November 1849. Cold weather and snow arrived before the company could build houses, so most of the families lived in dugouts that winter while a few lived in their wagons.

Not long after their arrival, Chief Joseph Walker and a band of approximately six hundred Indians came and pitched their tents about a mile away from the settlers. The Indians were friendly, but kept asking for food, which proved a hardship on the Saints as it pitifully reduced their already meager provisions.

Isaac Morley and the settlers at Manti got along, for the most part, very well with the Indians. Part of the reason for this was that the settlement was conceived largely as a mission to the Indians. Isaac wrote, "Did we come here to enrich ourselves in the things of this world? No. We were sent to enrich the Natives and comfort the hearts of the long oppressed. Let us try the experiment and if we fail to accomplish the object, then say, boys, come away."[16]

The first winter of 1849–1850 was a severe one. Because the Indians were suffering as well, Isaac allowed them to take and eat any of the settler's animals that had frozen to death. Still, food was so scarce that in January of 1850, despite the freezing cold and deep snow, Isaac had to send a group of men to Church headquarters to get food to prevent outright starvation.

Then, there was an outbreak of measles in the Sanpete area, which spread to the Indians. Chief Walker sent a message to Isaac, asking for help. Isaac left immediately to give the chief and twenty-four other Indians medical assistance. Although he helped save many lives, one of Chief Walker's sons died.

In writing about the measles outbreak to Brigham Young, Isaac remarked, "Walker says that the Sanpitches would all have died, and many of his men too, had we not been here." In the same letter, Isaac said that Chief Walker had told him, "I want the Mormons to stay here and plant and sow, and do us good, and we will be friends." Isaac added that the chief had sent word to all of the natives that were nearby "to stay at home and not to fight."[17]

In March, Father Morley wrote to President Young, reporting that during the winter, their group had lost forty-one oxen, thirty-eight cows, and three horses, along with fourteen head of stock, which the Indians had used for food. Brigham immediately sent ten loads of grain to help feed the settlers. During this time of trial, "Father Morley encouraged the suffering Saints by exhorting them to diligence, faithfulness in their individual and family prayers, and good works. Put the Lord to the test and receive the blessing earned, he would say. He made them believe that their settlement would one day be among the best in the mountains. Because of president Morley's courage and magnetic leadership, the Saints continued to unite their efforts and remained free from panic."[18]

As soon as weather permitted, the pioneers started building, and by mid-February, had erected twenty houses. By May, they had planted 250 acres of wheat, oats, barley, and potatoes. When the settlers became discouraged, Father Morley gently buoyed them up, telling them that one day, their little colony would be known as one of the best towns in all of Utah. His words were prophetic and, in time, the area became dotted with thriving villages; Manti, with its fertile fields and productive farms, became known as the granary of the Church.

It was around this time that problems arose between the settlers and Chief Walker, who demanded that Isaac give him his baby as a token of trust. But all was well when the chief returned the child unharmed.

On 4 August 1850, Brigham Young visited the settlement at Manti to give them advice and encouragement. Although Chief Joseph Walker had requested the presence of settlers, there had already been one crisis when the volatile Indian leader had threatened war. Brigham Young worried that the Utes might eventually become unhappy about the Mormons settling in their valleys. To prevent future problems and to show the Indians that the presence of the Mormons could mean a dependable food supply, Brigham appointed men to start a farming program among the natives.[19]

That fall, Isaac traveled to Salt Lake City. During general conference, he talked about the new settlement in Manti and the need for more settlers. Afterwards, Brigham spoke, saying, "I have it in my heart to ask the congregation if father Morley shall have the right and privilege to select such men as he wishes to go there." The assembly carried the motion and Isaac was allowed to choose one hundred men to augment the settlement.[20]

When Congress accepted Utah as a Territory on 9 September 1850, a provincial form of government was instituted. Isaac Morley and Charles Shumway were chosen to represent Sanpete County in the first Legislative Assembly. A year later, Manti was incorporated. By that time, Manti was a well-established livestock and agricultural center, with a population of approximately 365 people.[21]

Brigham wrote Isaac regularly and Isaac kept President Young informed of improvements in the settlement. On Brigham's second visit to Manti, he organized Sanpete into the fourth stake of Zion and called Isaac Morley to be its first Stake President. In addition to Isaac's ecclesiastical responsibilities, he also served as postmaster of Manti.[22]

In 1851, Isaac once again held a seat in the legislature. He was in Salt Lake City around Christmas, and at President Young's request, remained there during December to participate in holiday celebrations and attend to Church duties.[23]

As an influential member of the legislature, Isaac Morley helped pass a law prohibiting slave trade in 1852. One month after April's General Conference, President Young again stopped in Manti on his annual tour of the settlements. He invited Isaac to go with him to visit the settlements in southern Utah.[24]

That August, Brigham Young wrote Father Morley, asking him to invite Chief Walker to go to Salt Lake City and make a peace treaty with the Shoshones. Brigham wrote, "It is a good chance for Walker to come and make peace if he wants to, and I very much wish he would, but if he will not come, he must send his principal men and tell what he is willing to do. . . . Send us word forthwith Father Morley, in relation to this business so that we may know what to depend upon." Brigham ended by saying, "I have no more at present to write, but remain as ever your friend and brother in the gospel of Christ. Brigham Young."[25]

Unfortunately, the following year, conflicts arose and Chief Walker declared war on Brigham Young and the Mormons. Part of the problem appears to have stemmed from the chief's resentment over legislation that had been passed prohibiting slave trade. Although the war raged for several months in Utah and Salt Lake counties, it did not affect the pioneers in Manti. In April 1853, Brigham Young went to Manti to counsel the settlers about the conflict. During his visit, some Indians broke into the fort. They eluded the guards and managed to get to Isaac Morley's house, where they explained that Chief Walker had sent them to tell the Mormons that he wanted peace. Brigham then gave the Indians presents to take back to Chief Walker.[26]

Brigham was concerned about Father Morley's advancing age and worried that Isaac might decide he could no longer participate in the legislature, which was scheduled to assemble that December. Brigham wrote Isaac about this, saying, "I do not wish you to even dream of resigning . . . take your seat in the assembly." President Young added, "I have reflected upon your age, circumstances, and probably feelings and feel today that it would please me much if you would arrange your affairs with the view of returning and living with us here in this city at the earliest reasonable date."[27]

Cordelia Morley Cox, Isaac's daughter, explained why Brigham wanted Isaac to return to Salt Lake City: "The Indians were so hostile that President Young thought it too much for so old a man as father, so called him back to Salt Lake and furnished him a house to live in."[28]

Isaac went to Salt Lake City in mid-December and spoke to Church members at a conference. That afternoon, Brigham Young spoke on the principle of perfection, commenting that he applied that principle to himself and "to every man and woman upon the earth . . . including brother Morley who spoke to you this morning. . . . He has done the best he could in the latest Indian difficulties in the district where he lives, and acted according to the spirit of revelation in him, he is as justified as an angel of God!"[29]

Isaac returned to Manti long enough to settle up his affairs, and then moved to Salt Lake City. At the request of President Young, Father Morley began focusing exclusively on his duties as a patriarch.

At this time, John Smith was serving as Patriarch to the Church, with Isaac as an alternate. Although Isaac had not been a General Authority since his release from the Presiding Bishopric in 1840, whenever John Smith was not able to attend conference, Isaac Morley was listed as the

"Acting Church Patriarch" on the official rosters.[30]

In 1853, and again in 1855, Isaac was reelected a senator in the legislature. He finally resigned in 1857 so he could devote all of his time to his duties as a Church Patriarch.[31] Father Morley then moved to Fairview, Utah to live with his daughter, Lucy Diantha Allen.

Isaac Morley passed away on 24 June 1865. During his lifetime, Isaac showed himself to be a man of God. He was always a faithful, staunch friend of Brigham Young. His leadership abilities were indispensable as the Saints traveled west and began building up the Kingdom of God. Isaac played a key role in founding the settlement of Manti and in teaching the Indians the gospel. During the many years he served as a Patriarch, Isaac conferred blessings upon thousands of Saints.

"Isaac was a great leader because he was willing to follow, no matter how difficult the task or the risk to life, he obeyed his leader."[32]

Notes

1. Conway B. Sonne, *World of Wakara* (San Antonio: The Naylor Company, 1962), 157–58.

2. Ibid., 158–59.

3. Milton R. Hunter, *Brigham Young the Colonizer* (Santa Barbara: Peregrine Smith, Inc., 1941), 262.

4. B. H. Roberts, *A Comprehensive History of The Church of Jesus Christ of Latter-day Saints, Century One*, vol. 3, (Salt Lake City: Deseret News Press), 464.

5. John Clifton Moffitt, *Isaac Morley on The American Frontier* (unpublished manuscript on file at Salt Lake City: LDS Church History Library), 4.

6. Andrew Jenson, *Latter-day Saint Biographical Encyclopedia*, vol. 1 (Salt Lake City: Andrew Jenson History Company), 235.

7. Preston Nibley, *Exodus to Greatness: The Story of the Mormon Migration* (Salt Lake City: Deseret News Press, 1947), 36.

8. B. H. Roberts, ed., *History of The Church of Jesus Christ of Latter-day Saints, Period II*, from the Manuscript History of Brigham Young and Other Original Documents, vol. 7, (Salt Lake City: Deseret News, 1932), 543.

9. Robert Glass Cleland and Juanita Brooks, eds. *A Mormon Chronicle: The Diaries of John D. Lee 1848–1876*, vol. 2 (San Marino: The Huntington Library, 1955), 251.

10. Andrew Jenson, comp. *LDS Church Chronology 1805–1914*, revised by J. R. C. Nebeker (Orem: Quick and Easy Publishing, 2002), 35.

11. Eugene E. Campbell, *Establishing Zion, The Mormon Church in the American West, 1847–1869* (Salt Lake City: Signature Books, 1988), 33–34.

12. Leonard J. Arrington and Ronald K. Esplin, "The Role of the Council of the Twelve during Brigham Young's Presidency of The Church of Jesus Christ of Latter-day Saints," *Task Papers in LDS History*, No. 31 (Salt Lake City: History Division of the Historical Department of the LDS Church, Dec. 1979), 32.

13. Richard Henrie Morley, "The Life and Contributions of Isaac Morley," Master's Thesis, Brigham Young University (Copy on file at Salt Lake City: LDS Church History Library, 1965), 135.

14. *Journal History of the Church of Jesus Christ of Latter-day Saints*, 24 July 1849 (Salt Lake City: LDS Church History Library).

15. Campbell, *Establishing Zion, The Mormon Church in the American West, 1847–1869*, 66.

16. Dean L. May, *Utah: A People's History* (Salt Lake City: Bonneville Books, 1987), 104.

17. *Journal History of the Church of Jesus Christ of Latter-day Saints*, 20 February 1850, (Salt Lake City: LDS Church History Library).

18. Morley, *The Life and Contributions of Isaac Morley*, 154.

19. Ibid., 168.

20. Ibid., 170.

21. Wade Hendrickson, *The Settling of Manti* (Unpublished manuscript on file at Salt Lake City: LDS Church History Library), 8.

22. Morley, *The Life and Contributions of Isaac Morley*, 175.

23. Ibid., 183.

24. Ibid., 185.

25. Brigham Young, "Office files 1832–1878" (bulk 1844–1877), (Salt Lake City: LDS Church Archives).

26. Morley, *The Life and Contributions of Isaac Morley*, 188.

27. Ibid., 191–92.

28. Cordelia Morely Cox, *Brief History of Patriarch Isaac Morely and family 1907* (Unpublished document on file at Salt Lake City: LDS Church Archives), 5.

29. *Journal of Discourses*, 26 vols. (London, 1854–86), 130.

30. Morley, *The Life and Contributions of Isaac Morley*, 184.

31. Thomas Romney, *The Gospel in Action*, [Sunday School course of study, 1949], 118.

32. Ibid., 113.

Thomas Rhoades

1794–1869

There wasn't a person in Kamas, Utah, that didn't wonder where Thomas Rhoades[1] went when he suddenly disappeared, as he did from time to time. Although Thomas never told a soul where he was going, it wasn't long before neighbors found out he went into the mountains; but what he did there remained a mystery. It was certain Thomas wasn't hunting, for he never brought back any game. No, it was something else altogether, but no one knew exactly what it was, for Thomas refused to answer any questions or discuss anything regarding his secret expeditions. People were even more intrigued when they discovered that Thomas always went to Salt Lake City after one of his trips to the mountains.

The only thing Thomas would say about his trips was to tell people not to follow him, but this only added to the aura of mystery. Nearby settlers were obedient to his request, for not only was Thomas the ranking Mormon and military leader in the area, he also owned the land. Brigham Young himself had helped Thomas buy the land, so following him would be a clear-cut case of trespassing.

Thomas Rhoades's trips remained a mystery until years later when his son, Caleb, finally talked about them. The truth about the trips turned out to be even more surprising than anything anyone had imagined over the years.

Thomas Rhoades was born 13 July 1794 at Boone's Fort, Kentucky. He and his wife, Elizabeth, left Nauvoo with the Saints during the great exodus of 1846. Thomas became close friends with Brigham Young, who made Thomas captain over a large group.[2]

When food became scarce and sickness was prevalent among the homeless Saints, Thomas talked to Brigham Young to see what could be done to ease the suffering. Thomas said, "All the people are starving and freezing in this camp. Can't we at least move on to where there is food to be had, a place where we can build temporary shelters and fields where we can plant crops which will insure our next winter's food supply?"[3]

Brigham replied that he intended to do just that, but that he still had to gather the remnants of the people together, and with winter already upon them, the Saints could go no further until spring.

Thomas replied, "I have nearly 200 persons who will gladly follow me to wherever I may choose. Let me take them and go westward until I find a suitable place—I understand that California has much to offer in a good climate and soil—let me take these and blaze the trail west. Should I venture too far, I'll return when the settlement has been made."[4]

A council was held on 21 April 1846 to discuss the western migration, and during that meeting, Brigham and other leaders granted Thomas permission to take an exploration party to California. Thomas Rhoades and a group of approximately 250 people entered the Sacramento Valley on 5 October 1846.[5]

After settling in at Dry Creek, Thomas sent a letter to Brigham Young, informing him of their arrival. Thomas and a few others then went to work for Captain John Sutter. A short time later, his wife, Elizabeth, passed away. When Thomas remarried three years later, he began practicing polygamy.

When the Mormon Battalion arrived in San Diego in January 1847, some of the men stayed for a time to mine for gold. Then, gold was discovered at Sutter's Fort. Thomas and his sons were very successful at mining, and stayed until 1849, when a special courier from Salt Lake City delivered a letter to Thomas. The letter was from Brigham Young, who asked Thomas to return to Utah and bring any Mormons that were with him.[6]

At this time in Utah, the Saints were poverty stricken. Since there was very little money, most of the people traded for items they needed. However, as more people arrived in the valley, Church leaders saw a need to print currency and mint coins so that people had a means of exchange. The Church issued paper money against what little gold they had, but had little left over with which to mint coins. Although Brigham sent for professional equipment to print paper currency, the printing had to be halted because there was not enough gold to back the paper currency.

This deficiency was relieved somewhat when men from the Mormon Battalion, who had stayed in California to mine, went to Utah and paid their tithing and fast offerings with gold dust and nuggets. Some men freely gave the Church all the gold they had mined. In addition, Brigham asked a small number of trusted men to go to California on short-term missions to mine for gold.

In Church records, the "Gold Account" recorded how much gold was donated. Most of this gold was used for minting coins. Although accounts differ, it appears that Thomas Rhoades, who arrived in Salt Lake City at the end of September 1849, gave more gold to the Church than anyone else. According to the Gold Account, Thomas Rhoades was the only person who had a separate account in his own name. Everyone who donated gold, except for Thomas, had their contributions listed under Brigham Young's name. It was reported that Thomas brought a sixty-pound sack of gold to Salt Lake City, which was worth $16 an ounce at that time.[7]

On 9 October 1849, Thomas's account with the Church was credited with a deposit of $10,826 in raw gold, which was considered a fortune at that time.[8]

Brigham Young stated, "Before I had been one year in this place, the wealthiest man who came from the mines, Father Rhodes (Rhoads), with $17,000.00."[9]

According to Colonel Joseph M. Lock, "Father Rhodes brought several sacks of gold among which there was a 60-pound sack, the largest amount of gold that had been brought into the Valley. Father Rhodes turned all the gold over to Brigham Young, who in turn had a home built for Rhodes and allowed him to withdraw from the tithing office all the food supplies he deemed necessary . He also received a herd of cattle in consideration for the gold dust. Father Rhodes contributed the entire amount to accelerate the progress of the Mormon people. The famous 60-pound sack of gold was the chief topic of the people in the Valley at that time and for quite some time after."[10]

Because of the huge amount that Thomas donated, as well as many smaller donations by a large number of other men, the Church was able to begin minting coins and issuing one dollar bills in 1849.[11]

After his return to Utah, Thomas built a home in downtown Salt Lake City and became prominent in Church and civic affairs.[12]

In 1851, Thomas accompanied Brigham Young on his annual tour to the southern part of Utah. Thomas was later nominated as a county judge and named a school regent.[13]

A year later, during the first Territorial Legislature, Thomas Rhoades was named the first treasurer for Salt Lake County.[14]

In 1851, the flow of gold from California was suddenly and severely reduced, putting the Church in dire financial straits. Then, a miracle occurred, which saved the Saints from economic disaster. This miracle came about because of the friendship between Brigham Young and Chief Joseph Walker (sometimes called Wakara), the leader of the Ute Indians. When Brigham Young told Chief Walker about the financial difficulties the Saints were facing, Chief Walker said he wanted to help.

"Walker revealed to Brigham Young the presence of a yellow metal in the Uintah Mountains and agreed to let the Mormon church send someone in to get it out as needed. He set down three conditions that were to be met by Young:

1. The location of the gold would be known only by one man, to be chosen by Brigham Young. Brigham Young was not to know the location.
2. If the man chosen to get the gold from the Indians revealed the location, the penalty of death would be automatic. Any white man who attempted to follow the chosen man to locate the gold would also suffer death.
3. The Indians would not at any time assist in the mining of the gold."[15]

Utah folklore, as well as the Rhoades family history, identifies Thomas Rhoades as the man Brigham Young chose to go into the mountains and mine gold in order to build up Zion.

Brigham Young selected Thomas to fulfill this vital assignment for a number of reasons. "Rhoades was not only familiar with the Utes but friendly with them, and he was also their interpreter from time to time, therefore having an extensive knowledge of both their habits and their language. His days on the early frontiers of Kentucky and Illinois qualified him as an excellent backwoodsman . . . he was a qualified surveyor, and from the mining fields of California he brought his experience as a miner and goldsmith. And, there was no man in all Utah that Brigham Young trusted more."[16]

After agreeing to Chief Walker's three conditions, Brigham Young reportedly asked Chief Walker to swear an oath that he would not break his word and that Thomas Rhoades would be unharmed as he traveled in and out of Ute territory in the Uintah Mountains. Chief Walker promised that Thomas would be safe.

The money Thomas gleaned from the mines was used for noble purposes in helping the destitute Saints and in furthering the purposes of the Lord. Brigham used the money to support missionaries, help emigrants come west, and to build up new settlements throughout the Great Basin. It seems clear that greed played no play in the mining process, for Thomas only made approximately six or seven trips between 1852 and 1855. He mined enough to help the Church but not enough to make anyone rich. Thomas is reported to have gone on his first trip in 1852, with Chief Walker himself taking Thomas to the secret place.[17]

Thomas was gone fourteen days on his first trip, then—as became his custom—he took the gold directly to Brigham Young's home in Salt Lake City. Occasionally, Thomas took his son, Caleb, with him to the mountains, but Caleb was never allowed to go to the mine.

When newly-minted gold pieces began to appear in Salt Lake City, people began speculating as to their origin. Descendants of Thomas and Caleb Rhoades said that a rumor was started to cover up the source of this new gold. The rumor was that the coins were minted from gold donated by Thomas Rhoades when he came from California.[18]

Thomas was an experienced frontiersman and, at first, used his reputation as a trapper and hunter to cover his absences. Ephraim Lambert, who was a neighbor and close friend of Thomas Rhoades for many years, stated: "This man Rhoads came to Kamas Valley in the early days. . . . He spent a lot of time trapping and exploring . . . it was generally well known that he had discovered a rich gold mine somewhere east of Kamas. Nobody knew just where it was, but periodically he would make trips into the mountains and would come back with gold. . . . A lot of people saw it. My father saw it. He saw one sack full."

Apparently, Thomas was allowed to keep enough gold to sustain himself and his family as payment for his labors. Ephraim said, "Rhoads brought [the gold] to grandfather Lambert's place to have it weighed, so he would know how much tithing to pay on it. Grandfather had the only scales in town. . . . Now aside from what he needed for his own use, he gave the gold to the Mormon Church. He gave it to Brigham Young, and it was used to build the Salt Lake Temple."[19]

Although the mountains of Utah were filled with precious metals, President Young generally discouraged the Saints from mining such metals because he was fearful they might turn their hearts over to gold instead of the Lord. He explained, "We cannot eat silver and gold, neither do we want to bring to our peaceful settlements a rough frontier population to violate the morals of our youth, overwhelm us by numbers and drive us again from our hard earned homes."[20]

Brigham had good reasons for asking Thomas to keep his mission a secret. Ephraim Lambert said, "When Rhoads took that gold to Brigham Young, who was then Territorial Governor as well as Church President, Young told him never to make this thing public. The people then were farmers . . . so a gold mine like that would cause a stampede into the mountains and probably a lot of people would starve to death."[21] In addition, revealing the location of the gold mine would have resulted in a war with the Utes.

For three years, Thomas Rhoades faithfully carried out his mission, making one or two trips each year to the mountains and then to Salt Lake City to deliver the gold. Then, in June 1855, Thomas became ill. Chief Walker suggested that Thomas' son, Caleb, take over temporarily. Caleb agree, but before his first trip, he was asked to promise God, Brigham Young, and Chief Walker that he would never tell or show anyone where the gold was located.

"Then Brigham Young laid his hands on the head of Caleb and blessed him and set him apart the same as his father had been set apart. . . . Chief Walker selected a young Indian to act as guide and instructed him to protect Caleb from other Indians. . . . When they met other Indians, the guide would explain their mission and they went unmolested."[22]

When Chief Joseph Walker died in January 1855, his brother, Arropine, became the new leader of the Utes. On one of his visits to Brigham Young, Chief Arropine said that his brother had told him not to wage war with the Mormons and to cooperate with Brigham Young in retrieving more gold.[23]

When Thomas had fully recovered from his illness, he began going with Caleb into the Indian's land to mine, usually taking gifts. "The Utes thus became great friends of the two Rhoades, insomuch that they eventually accepted the both of them into the Ute tribe as full blood brothers."[24]

Because of the work Thomas was doing for the Church, Brigham Young helped him obtain a grant for a large tract of land upon which the mines were located, on the south slope of the Uintah Mountains. On 20 May 1857, Thomas Rhoades started a ranch at the site of what is now known as Kamas.[25]

During his expeditions, Thomas discovered several old Spanish mines. It is possible that some of the Indians who accompanied him showed him the location of these ancient mines.

In 1858, Thomas asked Brigham Young for permission to resign his position in the local government and begin a new settlement approximately fifty miles southeast of Salt Lake City. Thomas left with twenty-five men but the Ute Indians became highly offended when the settlers started building a stockade. Rather than upset the Indians, the men stopped their work and abandoned the valley.

Two years later, Thomas returned to the area and accidentally discovered a rich vein of coal while hunting game. "Using his hunting knife, he cut out samples, which he took to President Young."[26]

Brigham Young then asked Thomas to scout out new areas for settlements and in 1860, Thomas went as far east as the Uintah Basin. Thomas was also called to serve for a time as a missionary among the Yaqui Indians along the Colorado River.[27]

Based on the recommendations that Thomas gave him, Brigham Young sent families in the spring of 1861 to a new settlement that became known as Rhoades Valley (now Kamas).[28] The importance of Thomas Rhoades to the area is attested to by the many places named after him—for example, Rhodes Valley, Rhodes Plateau, Rhodes Peak, and Rhodes Creek.[29]

In 1862, Thomas was elected to serve in the Territorial Legislature as a representative from Summit County. When a post office was established in Kamas in 1864, Thomas became the first postmaster, even though he was sixty-nine years old. That same year, Thomas received a calling to develop some Church-owned mines near Minersville, and moved there.

Thomas Rhoades was seventy-four when he died in Minersville on 20 February 1869. After his father's death, Caleb made a few trips into the mountains to mine for gold. However, after Brigham Young died in 1877,

Chief Tabby, the new leader of the Utes, told the Mormons they could not have any more gold.

In 1898 or 1899, a party was given in the Town Hall at Price, Utah, to honor the old-timers. Robert Powell, a nephew of Caleb Rhoads, related that during the party, Caleb Rhoads was asked to talk about some of his experiences, since he was one of the oldest pioneers there. For the first time, Caleb spoke about the Rhoades Mine and his part in it.

Caleb said it had all started because his father, Thomas Rhoades, had been good friends with Brigham Young. Caleb explained that Brigham's gracious policy of feeding the Indians instead of fighting them had gained the trust and good will of the Indians—so much that they had told Brigham about a rich deposit of gold in the Uintah Mountains and had allowed him to assign a man to go in and get it.[30]

Caleb related the story, beginning with when his father had left California:

> One day, shortly after my father had returned from the gold fields of California, he met President Brigham Young on a street in Salt Lake City. "Brother Rhoades," President Young began, "you are the very man I've been looking for. I've a little mission for you—I want you to go into the Uintah Mountains to an old mine, with a guide that Chief Walker is going to appoint, and bring back as much gold ore as you can."
>
> On the appointed day, true to his promise, Chief Walker met President Young. With him he brought several hundred warriors, all gaily attired, a gesture which bespoke the importance that the noted war chief regarded the occasion. . . . That was in the beginning.
>
> Father made many trips, both to and from the old mine, without incident. Then, one summer, father was ill and couldn't go, and for some time Chief Aropene, [Occasionally, his name is written "Arrowpine"] who was then chief of the Utes, seemed to be mentally wrestling with the problem. Then his dark eyes snapped as if the answer had come. Pointing to me, he asked, "What about boy?" To which President Young nodded approval . . .
>
> Of me he requested that I hold up my right hand and vow before all present that I never would disclose the location of the mine to anyone as long as I lived. That oath I have never broken. We [Caleb and an Indian guide] went, and in due time returned with the ore. Thus, I fulfilled father's mission. I've been back since, and as long as President Young was alive the Indians proved friendly enough.[31]

Notes

1. The correct spelling of Thomas Rhoades is not known, as he spelled his name in various ways, such as Rhoads, Rhods, Rhodz, or even Roads. Since many of his descendants spell their name Rhoades, that is the spelling used here.

2. Norma Baldwin Ricketts, *Thomas and Elizabeth Rhoades, pioneers of 1846* (Salt Lake City: Unpublished manuscript on file at LDS Church Archives), 1–2.

3. Gale R. Rhoades, Kerry Ross Boren, *Footprints in the Wilderness, A History of The Lost Rhoades Mines* (Salt Lake City: Publisher's Press, 1971), 14.

4. Ibid., 13–14.

5. Ibid., 2–3.

6. Ibid., 45.

7. Ibid., 51.

8. George A. Thompson, *Faded Footprints, The Lost Rhoads Mines, and Other Hidden Treasures of Utah's Killer Mountains* (Salt Lake City: Roaming the West, 1991), 19.

9. Kate B. Carter, comp., *Our Pioneer Heritage*, vol. 9 (Salt Lake City: Daughters of Utah Pioneers, 1966), 478–79.

10. Ibid., 479.

11. Rhoades and Boren, *Footprints in the Wilderness, A History of The Lost Rhoades Mines*, 51.

12. Joseph Kenneth Davies, *Thomas Rhoads, Forgotten Mormon Pioneer of 1846* (Unpublished manuscript on file at LDS Church Archives), 89.

13. Ibid.

14. Ricketts, *Thomas and Elizabeth Rhoades, Pioneers of 1846*, 7.

15. Ibid., 7–8.

16. Rhoades and Boren, *Footprints in the Wilderness, A History of The Lost Rhoades Mines*, 67.

17. Thompson, *Faded Footprints, The Lost Rhoads Mines, and Other Hidden Treasures of Utah's Killer Mountains*, 20.

18. Rhoades and Boren, *Footprints in the Wilderness, A History of The Lost Rhoades Mines*, 69–70.

19. Thompson, *Faded Footprints, The Lost Rhoads Mines, and Other Hidden Treasures of Utah's Killer Mountains*, 23.

20. Rhoades and Boren, *Footprints in the Wilderness, A History of The Lost Rhoades Mines*, 76.

21. Thompson, *Faded Footprints, The Lost Rhoads Mines, and Other Hidden Treasures of Utah's Killer Mountains*, 24.

22. Kate B. Carter, comp., *Our Pioneer Heritage*, vol. 7, (Salt Lake City: Daughters of Utah Pioneers, 1964), 587.

23. Rhoades and Boren, *Footprints in the Wilderness, A History of The Lost Rhoades Mines*, 69.

24. Ibid., 71.

25. Thompson, *Faded Footprints, The Lost Rhoads Mines, and Other Hidden Treasures of Utah's Killer Mountains*, 20.

26. Carter, comp., *Our Pioneer Heritage*, vol. 7, 73.

27. Davies, *Thomas Rhoads, Forgotten Mormon Pioneer of 1846*, 92.

28. Rhoades and Boren, *Footprints in the Wilderness, A History of The Lost Rhoades Mines*, 78.

29. Davies, *Thomas Rhoads, Forgotten Mormon Pioneer of 1846*, 91.

30. Carter, comp., *Our Pioneer Heritage*, vol. 9, 479.

31. Rhoades and Boren, *Footprints in the Wilderness, A History of The Lost Rhoades Mines*, 119–20.

Thomas E. Ricks

1828–1901

Growing up on the borders of civilization, Thomas E. Ricks learned many survival skills that helped him meet the challenges of a hostile frontier while traveling to and starting a new life in the Salt Lake Valley. But all of the expertise in the world could not help Thomas when, while crossing the plains, he was shot three times by Indians and left for dead.[1]

Thomas was born 21 July 1828 in Kentucky. He was seventeen years old when he and his family were baptized and moved to Nauvoo. Thomas spent two years in Iowa and Winter Quarters before heading west in Heber C. Kimball's large company that consisted of 662 pioneers.[2]

Heber's company was camped at the Elkhorn River in June when Indians staged a morning raid, running off a number of cattle. Knowing that these cattle could mean the difference between survival or starvation for the Saints, Thomas E. Ricks and three other men went to find the missing cattle.

One account states:

> At 8 o'clock on the morning of June 6, 1848, an alarm sounded in the camp . . . Tom Ricks, Howard Egan, William Kimball, and Noah

Bartholomew jumped on their horses and traveled rapidly about six miles down the river.

They searched for the Indians in hopes of retrieving their livestock. Suddenly, they came upon a party of about ten Indians who immediately fired at them. Tom was hit with three rifle balls; two lodged in his kidneys and another hit his backbone. He fell from his horse and lay on the ground. The three friends of Tom, still on horseback, were driven away by the Indians. They turned and headed for the camp as rapidly as possible, leaving Tom on the ground, presumably dead or dying.

Looking back as they fled, they saw one Indian moving toward Tom . . . intending to scalp him.[3]

When Howard, William, and Noah returned to camp, they told Thomas's father that his son had been shot. He then took a wagon across the river to search for his son's body. His joy at discovering that his son was still alive quickly turned to panic when he saw that Thomas was badly wounded.

Thomas's father floated his son across the river on a buffalo hide, and then used his wagon to carry him back to camp. Thomas was so critically wounded that the doctor felt that surgery to remove the rifle balls would certainly kill him. The doctor dressed the wounds, saying that Thomas could not live more than a few hours. Then Heber C. Kimball came to see what could be done.

"Bro. Kimball administered to him and promised him in the name of the Lord that he should recover and live to see the Latter-day saints become a mighty people in the midst of the Rocky Mountains."[4]

When Thomas was able to speak, the men asked what had happened to stop the Indian they had seen raising his arm to scalp him. Thomas explained that when the Indian approached, he had put up an arm to protect himself, badly startling the Indian, who thought Thomas was dead. The Indian then left abruptly without carrying through with his plans.

"Years later, Thomas, speaking at a family reunion, told of a special spiritual experience that comforted him as he lay on the ground [after being shot]: 'While I lay there weltering in blood, I thought of the condition of my father and family and how badly they needed my assistance in crossing the plains and making a home in a new land and wondered if I was going to die.

"While thus engaged in thought, I heard a voice say audibly and clearly, 'You will not die; you will go to the valley of the mountains and there you will do a great work in your day and generation.' "[5]

As Heber C. Kimball promised, Thomas did live and by the time the company arrived in Salt Lake City on 24 September 1848, he had nearly recovered from his wounds. Thomas made his home at Mill Creek, a few miles north of Salt Lake City and the following year moved to Centerville.

In the summer of 1849, Thomas was sent with Ezra T. Benson, George A. Smith and a group of other men to take wagons to Independence Rock, Wyoming and assist a company of Norwegian immigrants that were having difficulties.

In November, Brigham Young called Thomas and forty-nine other men to go on an exploring expedition, under Apostle Parley P. Pratt, to southern Utah to find sites for new settlements. Thomas traveled over seven hundred miles during this mission, mapping out locations for future colonies.

While on this mission, Thomas and a few other men were exploring when it began to snow. After traveling for twenty days, Parley P. Pratt decided they could not make it back to their base camp before they ran out of food. It was decided that half of the men should camp where they were, while the other half went on to Provo, which was one hundred miles away. Those that went to Provo had to travel through snow that was three to four feet deep. One man would break the trail while the others followed, and when he became tired, another man would take his place. Thomas was one of those who remained behind, camping among shrub cedars, which provided some shelter for their animals.[6]

Thomas returned home in March 1850. Two years later, he married Tabitha Hendricks on 28 August 1852. Later, he married other wives.

When President Young felt it would be useful to develop a settlement halfway between Salt Lake City and California, he called Thomas E. Ricks and twenty-nine other frontiersmen to this mission at Las Vegas, Nevada, during General Conference in April of 1855.[7]

With William Bringhurst as the leader, the group of missionaries left on 10 May 1855, for their 435 mile trip. They had forty wagons pulled by oxen, fifteen cows, and a number of horses. It was a difficult journey. One day, it took six yoke of oxen and twenty men to pull a single wagon up a hill in the hot sun. Another time, the men had to cross fifty-two miles of desert without any water. During the last ten days of their journey, daytime temperatures often reached as high as 115 degrees, forcing the elders to travel mostly at night.[8]

The missionaries arrived in Las Vegas in June. Their primary goals were to establish a settlement, begin farming, build a fort, and construct a bowery where they could hold meetings. They had also been directed to make friends with the Indians. George Washington Bean proved helpful with this, as he had been sent to act as an interpreter. George told the local Indians that the great chief, Brigham Young, had sent them there to do good and to teach them how to raise corn and other crops.

The elders asked the Indians for permission to use some of their land and made a peace treaty, which promised that the missionaries would treat the Indians well and asked that the Indians treat them the same way.

In one of his letters to his wife, Tabitha, Thomas wrote, "It is with pleasure that I sit down to write a few lines to you. . . . I can say, as you have said, that I never tried harder to do what is right than I have on this mission . . . I feel all right about being here because I know it is the will of my Heavenly Father. It is also for my salvation and yours and peradventure for the salvation of the Lamanites . . . as for this mission, it is but of momentary concern but I do expect that from this time forth my time will be spent in the work of the Lord, throughout time and all eternity. That is my desire and determination."[9]

Although Brigham told the missionaries they could go home for the winter, Thomas stayed in Las Vegas, feeling he was needed there. Sixteen other missionaries remained and Thomas said they made great progress in befriending the thousand Indians that lived nearby. During the winter, the missionaries developed a school where they could learn and educate themselves.

The following year, more missionaries were sent to the area. Unfortunately, a division arose and they split into two sides. Each side had a spokesman who appealed to Brigham Young for counsel. President Young decided to temporarily close the mission. Thomas was released on 24 September 1856 and returned home with George Washington Bean.

Thomas had only been home ten days when, during General Conference in October 1856, he was called to go help the handcart companies that had become trapped by early snowstorms. Thomas met the Martin Handcart Company at Independence Rock and assisted them until they arrived in Salt Lake City on 30 November 1856.

President Brigham Young thought highly of the young men who had gone to help rescue the handcart pioneers. He said, "Every boy that has gone out to save those handcart pioneers and endured that cold and frost and snow and those frozen rivers; every one of those boys will be saved in the celestial kingdom of God."[10]

In the spring of 1857, Thomas left again to help another handcart company. This one arrived in Salt Lake City on 12 September 1857, and was one of the last companies to travel by handcart. Then, in March 1858, Thomas was sent to Salmon River, Idaho to rescue Thomas S. Smith's company from Indians.

A crisis occurred during 1857–1858 when President James Buchanan believed unsubstantiated reports that stated the people of Utah were rebelling against the United States Government. President Buchanan dispatched an army to Utah to put down the rebellion and to install—forcibly if necessary—a new governor, Alfred Cumming. Remembering the severe persecution the Saints had received at the hands of mobs, with no protection from government, Brigham turned to the Nauvoo Legion (also known as the Utah Militia) for help in defending the Saints. Thomas was one of those who were called into action.

Edward Tullidge wrote, "(Lieutenant) Thomas E. Ricks was called into the field as one of the most reliable men in the Territory. In September 1857, he went out with Lieutenant General D. H. Wells to meet Johnston's army."[11]

Brigham asked his friend Colonel Thomas L. Kane to meet with the army and federal officials at Camp Scott and try to negotiate a peaceful settlement. When Governor Cumming and other federal officials agreed to meet personally with President Young, Thomas E. Ricks and a few other men were sent to escort the men to Salt Lake City.

By prearrangement with Porter Rockwell, Lot Smith and a few other leaders, the militia made bonfires at various places in the canyon. Groups of men stopped the officials at these points. After questioning the officials, the Mormons would allow them to continue their journey before hastily mounting up and riding on to the next stop to wait for the officials. The men would keep their faces concealed as much as possible, so as to not be recognized. In this way, the Mormons made the federal officials think there were vast numbers of men prepared to fight the incoming army should they choose to march on to Salt Lake City. This tactical maneuver persuaded the officials that the army could never get through the canyon because it was so heavily guarded and that it would be necessary to negotiate a settlement.

Once Governor Cumming arrived in Salt Lake City and was received by Brigham Young and other leaders, he sent a message to Washington, saying that he and the other officials had been cordially received and that the Mormons were not in revolt. The crisis then ended.

Thomas R. Ricks went to Cache Valley in the fall of 1859 with a group of settlers and began a new settlement, which was called Logan. After their arrival, most of the Saints stayed in tents while others slept in wagons. Cooking was done over open campfires, and they baked bread in wooden ovens they had brought with them. Water had to be carried from the river, and wood from the nearby forests.[12]

The settlers began building log cabins immediately. Most of the cabins had no windows and only dirt for floors. A few families had to hang a quilt over the door opening as a makeshift door, even in the winter. It was unlikely that any of the houses ever stayed dry in the winter and it was reported that some people had to take umbrellas to bed to stay dry during the night.[13]

Money was scarce in the new settlement. Thomas's wife hired one woman for one dollar a week, allowing her to earn enough money to buy wheat seed to plant. Despite their poverty, the settlers managed to build a school and a bowery.

Thomas E. Ricks served as a leader in Cache Valley from 1859–1883. He was a member of the high council for many years and also served as Presiding Bishop of Cache Valley. He met regularly with bishops to offer guidance and counsel, since most bishops served without counselors.

The pioneers had to protect their farm animals not only from wolves and bitter cold but from cattle rustling by the Indians. It was Brigham's policy to have the Saints feed the Indians rather than fight them, and while this policy was usually successful, a few Indians still took the settler's livestock.

This became an ongoing problem and finally, the men organized a branch of the militia on 29 April 1860. They called themselves "Minute Men" because they could respond to a call for help with only a minute's notice. The Minute Men had two groups—cavalry and infantry. As a lieutenant, Thomas E. Ricks was appointed to lead the cavalry, which consisted of over one thousand men.[14]

From 1861 to 1863, Thomas served as a Cache County sheriff. While Thomas was living in Logan, Brigham Young asked him on three separate occasions to go to Omaha, a distance of one thousand miles, and bring immigrants across the plains to Utah.[15] On his first trip to Omaha in 1863, Thomas was captain of a group that took wagons, teams, and provisions to Nebraska. He brought back a company of seventy-five wagons and five hundred English and Welsh Saints to Salt Lake City.

A few years later, on 5 July 1866, Thomas went back to Nebraska and brought back 230 emigrants. They were followed by a mule train, with forty-six wagons.[16]

In 1869, Thomas was called during the October General Conference to serve a short-term mission in the east. He was told to try to counteract prejudice and encourage good feelings toward the Church. He was given two weeks to make preparations and left in October to serve in Ohio, Illinois, and Kentucky.

On 17 May 1877, Brigham Young traveled to Logan to choose a site for a new temple. Around this time, Thomas E. Ricks became a railroad entrepreneur. He was one of the principal contractors chosen to build the railroad from Ogden, Utah, to Franklin, Idaho. Brigham Young passed away in the fall of 1877 and that same year, Thomas was awarded the contract to lay track from Franklin, Idaho to Butte, Montana. In 1881, Thomas worked as a contractor for the Northern Pacific Railroad.

In 1883, President John Taylor called Thomas Edwin Ricks and a group of other men to colonize the upper Snake River. Even though Thomas was living in Logan at the time, he was called to be the bishop of the Bannock Ward in Idaho. A year later, in February 1884, Thomas was called as the new stake president of the Bannock Stake.

Thomas and his family arrived in Idaho on 11 January 1883. After Thomas and others selected the site for a settlement, it was suggested it be named Rexburg in honor of Bishop Thomas Ricks—Rex being the German equivalent of the name Ricks.[17]

Thomas worked hard to build up the area. Not only did he help lay out settlements, he built the first grist mill in the upper Snake River valley, the first ferry across the north fork of the Snake River, and the first saw mill. He also established a flour mill and helped build canals for irrigation.

The new settlers were very poor, and when supplies were short, Thomas built a store and gave everyone credit. For a long time, he bore a large part of the colony's expenses. "When his resources were exhausted, he turned to his influential friends and induced them to help."[18]

Giving credit so freely resulted in his financial ruin. Although he had been a wealthy man while contracting for railroads, Thomas used all his money to help develop the Snake River country and assist the poor and needy. When Thomas could not pay his bills, creditors took his businesses, one after the other. Then, his mills were destroyed by fire. Even with all of his losses, Thomas said, "I was called here and have expended my means for the benefit of the people.... My means have been used up, and I am comparatively poor. But my faith has been increased in the Lord, and I acknowledge the blessings of the Lord."[19]

Andrew Jenson said of Thomas: "The savings and accumulations of a great many years of industrious toil were all spent through his kindness and liberality."[20]

The settlers were having such a difficult time that some of them considered leaving the struggling community to go elsewhere. However, Thomas encouraged them to stay, and many did. One man said, "Thomas E. Ricks and his associates accomplished more in two years in building canals, fences, bridges, and making general improvement that I have ever known of in the course of five years.... Thomas E. Ricks was an excellent manager."[21]

In 1885, Thomas left to serve a two-year mission to England. When he returned, there were a number of people who had moved to the area that were unfriendly toward the Saints. Because of this, it was decided to set up a Mormon educational institution. Thomas Ricks worked with Church leaders, and Bannock Stake Academy was established at Rexburg on 12 November 1888. It's name was changed various times and though it started as an elementary school, it eventually became a college. On 5 March 1902, the First Presidency suggested naming it Ricks Academy in honor of Thomas E. Ricks.[22]

On 21 June 2000, President Gordon B. Hinckley announced that Ricks College would be renamed Brigham Young University-Idaho. However, Church leaders wanted to honor Thomas E. Ricks, and Elder David A. Bednar announced that a new facility and the nearby demonstration gardens would be named the Thomas E. Ricks Building and Gardens. During this announcement, Elder Bednar stated, "It is most appropriate that this new academic building and beautiful garden area bear the name of Thomas E. Ricks as a lasting tribute to his valiant and pioneering educational efforts."[23]

Thomas E. Ricks, founder of towns, church buildings, schools, and a builder of bridges, canals, and railroad lines, died at his home in Rexburg, Idaho, on 28 September 1901. At the time of his death, his horses were hitched to a buggy and were waiting outside his home to take him to yet another church meeting.[24]

Thomas E. Ricks was a pioneer, lawman, missionary, and a business and religious leader—a man of great faith who had a resolute determination to serve the Lord and his Church. Throughout his long life, he devoted himself to colonizing the rugged environment and establishing a temporal and spiritual society in the Rocky Mountains. "He was a strong and determined leader and yet he was also a humble follower, willing to accept any calling from his own leaders in pursuit of a great cause."[25]

Hundreds of people attended Thomas' funeral. Schools were closed, flags flew at half mast, and businesses were closed one hour before and after the burial. At Thomas' funeral, President Rulon S. Wells of the first Quorum of Seventy said that Thomas "was one of those who would sacrifice all, even life itself, to the principle of truth to which he was firmly attached."[26]

Speaking at the funeral, President Joseph F. Smith added, "It may be a long time before we find another man his equal in honor, mind, and unswerving loyalty to the cause of God and His people."[27]

As a final tribute, historian Andrew Jenson said, "Those who knew him best assert that a more courageous man never lived than Thomas E. Ricks; for fear to him was unknown. . . . To the kingdom of God, and the Priesthood, he was loyal to the core, ever ready and willing to go where he was called and when he was called, unflinchingly braving every danger and hardship without a murmur. His was a cheerful disposition and he always had words of encouragement to those who were laboring to build up the new country in which he took so much interest."[28]

Notes

1. Steven D. Bennion, "Thomas E. Ricks," *Pioneer*, Autumn 2001, 12–17.

2. Ibid.

3. Ibid., 15.

4. Wanda Ricks Whyler, *Thomas E. Ricks, Colonizer and Founder*, 2nd ed. (Provo: M.C. Printing, 1989), 15.

5. Bennion, "Thomas E. Ricks," 15.

6. Whyler, *Thomas E. Ricks, Colonizer and Founder*, 2nd ed., 27.

7. Evelyn Ricks, "Thomas E. Ricks, a Founding Father," *Snake River Echoes*, vol. 5, issue 1, 1976, 14.

8. Whyler, *Thomas E. Ricks, Colonizer and Founder*, 2nd ed., 30.

9. Ibid., 33.

10. Bennion, "Thomas E. Ricks," 16.

11. Whyler, *Thomas E. Ricks, Colonizer and Founder*, 2nd ed., 51.

12. Ibid., 59.

13. Ibid., 60.

14. "True Cache Valley Pioneers," *Pioneer*, Autumn 1999, 22.

15. Ricks, "Thomas E. Ricks, a Founding Father," 15.

16. Whyler, *Thomas E. Ricks, Colonizer and Founder*, 2nd ed., 15, 92.

17. Bennion, "Thomas E. Ricks," 17.

18. Ricks, "Thomas E. Ricks, a Founding Father," 16.

19. "Thomas E. Ricks, A Man of Foresight," *Ensign*, Oct. 2001, 36.

20. Andrew Jenson, *Latter-day Saint Biographical Encyclopedia*, vol. 1, four volumes (Salt Lake City: Andrew Jenson History Company, 1901), 457.

21. Whyler, *Thomas E. Ricks, Colonizer and Founder*, 2nd ed., 140.

22. Bennion, "Thomas E. Ricks," 17.

23. Rachel Ludlow, "Preserving the Memory of Thomas E. Ricks," *Summit Magazine*, volume 10, issue 1 (Spring 2005), 10.

24. Whyler, *Thomas E. Ricks, Colonizer and Founder*, 2nd ed., 178.

25. Ibid., 1.

26. Ibid., 2.

27. "Thomas E. Ricks, A Man of Foresight," 36.

28. Jenson, *Latter-day Saint Biographical Encyclopedia*, 457.

Orrin Porter Rockwell

1813–1878

Orrin Porter Rockwell, who usually went by the name of Porter Rockwell, was a fearless scout, pioneer, sheriff, and one of the most famous frontiersmen of his time. Porter served as a bodyguard to both Joseph Smith and Brigham Young. President Brigham Young often asked Porter to safeguard him and other leaders of the Church as they traveled to and from settlements in Utah. In carrying out his duties as a sheriff, Porter was constantly called on to face dangerous criminals. His participation in the Utah War and extraordinary skill at tracking added to his fame.

There are scores of stories about Porter Rockwell, many of which have blended and changed through the years so that it is hard to know which have their basis in fact. However, there is no doubt that Porter Rockwell was a colorful and picturesque character. He cared little about the amenities of society, wore his hair long, swore often, and in his later years, often drank liquor. However, Porter was also honest, always willing to help others, and completely loyal to the prophets he served so diligently.

In 1870, Fitz Hugh Ludlow, a writer, described Porter Rockwell:

> His figure was of the middle height, and very strongly made; broad

across the shoulders, and set squarely on the legs. His arm of large girth, his chest round as a barrel, and his hand looked as powerful as a grizzly bear's. His face was of the mastiff type, and its expression, fidelity, fearlessness, ferocity. A man with his massive lower jaw, firm mouth, and good-humored but steady and searching eyes of steel-blue. . . . His hair, black and iron-gray in streaks, was gathered into a cue, just behind the apex of the skull, and twisted into a hard round bunch, confined with a comb. . . . He was very obliging in his manners.[1]

George W. Bean, who often accompanied Porter on missions to the Indians, said of him, "He was above average height, quick in movement, with strong arms and chest, and gray eyes—cool and searching. . . . He was demanding, yet kind and tender. . . . In our missionary work, he was humble and earnest. We spent many years of dangerous and worthwhile service together in teaching . . . and in aiding the officials of Government to subdue and punish outlaws. Anyone who really does something worthy of attention, is often misunderstood and misrepresented."[2]

Orrin Porter Rockwell was born in Belcher, Massachusetts, on 28 June 1813. He had no education and, as an adult, was unable to read or write. His family was friendly with Joseph Smith's family and after Joseph's vision, when many friends turned against the Smiths, the Rockwell family remained loyal and supportive. Porter was one of Joseph's especial friends. In the evenings, after Porter's chores were done, he would gather and sell wood and even pick berries by moonlight to earn money, which he then gave to Joseph to assist in printing the Book of Mormon.[3]

Porter Rockwell was baptized on 6 April 1830, the same day the Church was officially organized. Two years later, on 2 February 1832, Porter married Luana Beebee.

Along with the rest of the Saints, Porter faced much persecution; in January 1834, a raging mob destroyed his home. One of Porter's neighbors, Mr. Pettegrew, reported, "They threw his [Porter's] house down, or all they could, cut open feather beds, destroyed all of his furniture and all they could lay hands on."[4]

Porter's experience with mobs seemed to have had a great effect on him. His friend, George W. Bean, said that Porter "was always well armed since his Nauvoo experiences, although the Prophet Joseph told him to wear his hair long and he would never be killed by an enemy."[5]

Porter was always a true friend to the Prophet Joseph Smith. In December of 1838, when Joseph spent five months in Liberty Jail, Porter faithfully took him and the other brethren food and drink.[6] By October 1839, Porter had gained a reputation as a sharpshooter. After having proven his loyalty and courage, he was chosen to protect Joseph Smith.

When Governor Lilburn W. Boggs was shot and severely wounded in May of 1842, Joseph Smith and Porter Rockwell were implicated by anti-Mormon newspapers. However, in an affidavit, John C. Bennet testified that Porter told him that "he had been wrongfully accused of wishing to assassinate him, [Boggs] or of being ordered by Smith to do so." When John said he thought Joseph had ordered Porter to kill Boggs, Porter replied that "Smith had never given [me] any such orders, neither was it his intention to have [me] kill Boggs."[7] Although Porter was miles away at the time of the shooting, a warrant was issued for his and Joseph's arrest and they went into hiding.

During this time, Joseph did a lot of writing. Once, he mentioned that he wanted to list his friends, but that they were too numerous to be written. Joseph then added, "But there is one man I would mention, namely Orrin Porter Rockwell, who is now a fellow-wanderer with myself, an exile from his home, because of the . . . unrelenting hand of the Missourians. He is an innocent and a noble boy. May God Almighty deliver him from the hands of his pursuers. He was an innocent and noble child and my soul loves him."[8]

Fearing that if he was captured in Missouri, he would not get a fair trial, Porter went east for a time, but after his return, was arrested for the shooting of Governor Boggs. Porter was put in irons and kept in a dungeon, with only a little dirty straw for a bed, vile food to eat, and no way to keep warm in very cold weather. It was around this time that his wife, Luana, left him.

Despite these troubles, Porter stayed loyal to the Church and to his friend, Joseph. Once, he was asked to betray Joseph Smith. "On one occasion Sheriff Reynolds said [to Porter]: 'We know the Prophet has great confidence in you. Allure him [Joseph] to a place where we can arrest him and you shall have your freedom and any pile of money you name.' Porter Rockwell, weak and so emaciated that he could hardly stand, never faltered in his fidelity to his Prophet friend. His eagle eyes flashed and he blurted out in defiance. 'I'll see you all in hell first, and then I won't.' "[9]

When Porter was finally brought to trial, after spending nearly nine months in prison, the case was dismissed because of lack of evidence. Porter started immediately for Nauvoo, arriving at Joseph's home on

Christmas day in 1843. When Porter tried to enter, guards blocked his way. The Prophet, hearing the commotion, pushed through to see a dirty, raggedly man with long hair grinning at him. Joseph wrote, "To my great surprise and joy untold, I discovered it was my long-tried, warm, but cruelly persecuted friend, Orrin Porter Rockwell, just arrived from nearly a year's imprisonment, without conviction, in Missouri."[10]

The death of Joseph Smith in 1844 affected Porter greatly. Nearly two years after Joseph Smith's death, when Porter saw young Joseph, the thirteen-year old son of the dead Prophet, he broke down and wept. Young Joseph wrote about this, saying, "[Porter] put an arm affectionately around my shoulders, and said, with much emotion, 'Oh, Joseph, Joseph! They have killed the only friend I have ever had!' He wept like a boy."[11]

The Saints were preparing to leave Nauvoo when Porter was arrested on a different charge. The charge was eventually dropped, but since Porter had no money to pay his lawyer, Almon W. Babbit, he was forced to give Almon his gold watch. After returning to Nauvoo in January 1846, Porter received his endowments in the Nauvoo temple. As the Saints left the city, Brigham assigned Porter to transport messages along the eight pioneer camps that were stretched across Iowa.[12]

That August, Brigham asked Porter to be his bodyguard. When Porter happened to mention his giving Almon Babbit his watch as payment for his legal fees, Brigham became indignant and immediately fired off a letter, telling Almon that the Church property they had left in Nauvoo was sufficient to meet all of Porter's expenses and that he wanted Babbit to return Porter's watch immediately.[13]

On 14 April 1847, the first group of pioneers headed west. As a skilled frontiersman, Porter was appointed scout and chief hunter. Once the pioneers arrived in the Salt Lake Valley, Brigham realized that irrigation was their only hope of raising crops in the dry valley. He asked Porter to explore the mountains and survey irrigation possibilities. After that assignment, Brigham had Porter organize hunting and tree-hauling expeditions. That fall, Brigham Young asked Porter to go to Winter Quarters with him and a few of the brethren. Porter acted as a scout, hunter, and also protected the brethren from Indian attacks.

On 29 March 1849, Porter Rockwell was appointed a Deputy Marshal[14] for the provisional State of Deseret. [15]

Porter served as a peace officer for the rest of his life and in the course of his duties, often risked his life to capture outlaws. "He was brave, quick-witted, and always prepared. In the course of his duties he captured a large number of dangerous criminals and delivered them to the proper authorities."[16]

One of Brigham Young's top priorities after arriving in the Great Salt Lake Valley was to live in peace with the Indians. To achieve this, Brigham sought out dependable men who could speak the Indian's language and who had proven themselves able to get along well with the Indians. Porter was one of a handful of men who had great success with the Indians. Brigham Young designated Porter Rockwell and George W. Bean as two of his official interpreters. Brigham relied on these two intrepid frontiersmen to resolve conflicts among the Indians, even though they were often in great danger.[17]

The Indians respected Porter and came to trust him because he understood their needs and was always fair with them. His talent was recognized when the High Council announced that Porter Rockwell was one of only three men allowed to trade with the Indians on behalf of the Saints.[18]

One time, Brigham sent Porter and George W. Bean to Utah Valley to try and negotiate a cessation of hostilities that had recently erupted with the Ute Indians. George refused to carry a weapon, even though the trouble was so serious that the Indians were wearing war paint and actively preparing for war. Porter, on the other hand, was a walking arsenal—loaded down with a rifle, two revolvers, and a bowie knife. When the two men were able to reach a peaceful resolution and returned to Salt Lake City to report to the Prophet, George said, "Brother Brigham was pleased to know our experiences and told us to continue our mission to all the Tribes and make sure they understood our purpose in coming here was to build homes, raise cattle and grain, and teach them."[19]

Porter and George spent many years working together as missionaries and peacemakers. George said of his friend: "Orrin Porter Rockwell as I knew him, was a diamond in the rough. It was great to know his inner self. His honest loyalty to Church, Country and friends was deep and lasting. He abhorred deceit and intrigue as did I. He knew the need and power of prayer, as did I."[20]

When Colonel Steptoe, the commander over United States troops in Salt Lake City, asked Brigham Young for help in finding the Indians who were responsible for murdering eight railroad surveyors, President Young offered him the services of Porter Rockwell and George Bean. The two men were given an escort of twenty soldiers, and after meeting with Indian chiefs, were able to resolve the situation.

In April 1849, Brigham Young asked Porter Rockwell to act as a guide for Apostle Amasa Lyman, who was going to California. After they arrived, Amasa went to deliver an epistle to the Saints and to collect tithing while Porter went to dig gold. Having little success, Porter decided instead to open a saloon and two traveler's inns.[21]

In September of 1850, Porter left his businesses behind when he was asked to lead Charles C. Rich and a group of fifty-one men to Salt Lake City. Because of Porter's skills, not one man was lost, even though large bands of Indians followed them for nearly four hundred miles.[22]

Porter's unique lifestyle contributed to many legends and he often found himself the center of controversy and strange tales. Although many of the stories were without foundation, they still flourished. While some admired his steadfast loyalty to Brigham Young, others disliked him for his drinking and harsh language. Ever since he had been accused of shooting Governor Boggs, enemies continued to blame him for a number of unsolved incidents. However, one of Porter Rockwell's neighbors, Israel Bennion, vouched for Porter's character, saying: "As a neighbor ranchman, I have partaken of his hospitality, have ridden with him on the range, have noted the sagacity and skill with which he directed the breeding and feeding of his herds. I have been edified by accounts of my father of his neighborly relations with this old friend, from before my time. And so I bear my testimony to the honorable character of Orrin Porter Rockwell."[23]

Brigham Young was one of those who trusted Porter. In June 1851, Brigham Young called Porter into his office. Although the specifics of that meeting are not recorded, Porter was probably assigned once again as a missionary to the Indians, along with George W. Bean, since they both spent the next few months with the Indians.[24]

Then came the disastrous Walker War, which pitted white settlers against Chief Joseph Walker and his band of Ute Indians. In 1854, Brigham Young became determined to heal the ill feelings that had led up to this war and resulted in many deaths and widespread destruction of property. To improve relationships, President Young sent Porter Rockwell, George Washington Bean, and a few other men to meet Chief Walker at Chicken Creek in Utah. The Prophet told the men to do everything possible to restore trade with the Utes and to teach them agriculture and husbandry. He added that it was their special assignment to keep peace with Chief Walker, even if it took as much as $10,000 from the Church treasury to spend on cattle and other gifts for the Indians.

George related, "The President privately told us to keep peace with the Indians at all costs this season, as the people had suffered so much the last year by the Walker War that this year they must raise their crops."[25]

During the talks in April, Chief Walker sent word that he wanted to talk to President Young in person and that if Brigham brought plenty of cattle, flour, and other goods, all would be well. In response, Brigham Young and other Church leaders such as Heber C. Kimball, Wilford Woodruff, John Taylor, Ezra T. Benson, Lorenzo Snow, and others, set out for Chicken Creek with up to one hundred wagons filled with supplies for the Indians.[26]

At this meeting, Brigham told Chief Walker that he would send Porter Rockwell, George Bean, and others to trade with the Utes and keep them supplied with goods without Chief Walker having to go to Salt Lake City.[27]

On 3 May 1854, Porter married Mary Ann Neff. Brigham Young, his friend, performed the ceremony. The very next day, Porter left to accompany Brigham Young on his annual tour to southern Utah to visit settlements.

In 1855, Colonel Steptoe asked Porter Rockwell to go with him and scout out a route to Carson Valley. The quartermaster of the expedition wrote, "As a matter of security, another party was organized under 'Porter Rockwell,' a Mormon, but a man of strong mind and independent spirit, a capital guide and fearless prairie-man."[28]

Porter obviously made a good impression, for the next time Colonel Steptoe went to California, he personally asked Porter to go with him again as a guide for the United States Calvary. While he was in California, Porter visited a widow, Agnes Smith—a niece of Joseph Smith. When Porter saw that Agnes, who was recovering from typhoid fever, had lost all her hair, he wanted to help, but had no money. He then cut his long hair and gave it to her so she could make a wig.[29]

In 1855, two French scientists, Jules Remy and Julius Brenchley, stopped in Salt Lake City and spent some time with Porter. Remy wrote:

> He [Porter] is a man without much education . . . but at the same time extremely amiable and polite, with exceedingly distinguished and graceful manners. . . . He has been accused, on no evidence—and many still persist in accusing him—of having, in May, 1842, fired a pistol at Governor L. W. Boggs, of Missouri. . . . What appears clear

to us is, that Rockwell is incapable of doing wrong except under the impression that he is doing right; so persuaded are we of this, that we would trust him with life and property without any hesitation. He is a lion in a lamb's skin, that we admit; but a brave and generous lion, full of heart and greatness . . . ready to sacrifice himself in behalf of any one who has gained his esteem, without exception of sect or person . . . He is of the stuff from which heroes are wrought.[30]

When Brigham Young won a mail service contract with the government in 1857, he asked Porter to ride the first leg of the journey, which was between Salt Lake City and Fort Laramie. On Porter's first ride, he brought back twenty-four sacks of mail bound for Salt Lake City—the first delivery of mail from the east in nearly six months. The local newspaper wrote, "The Eastern mail arrived on the 29th, having left Independence on the 1st of May, and much credit is due to Mr. John Murdock, conductor to Laramie, and to Mr. O. P. Rockwell, conductor from that point to this city, for the perseverance, prudence and energy displayed in the transportation of so large a mail in such good time and condition."[31]

Porter was in Wyoming that same year when he learned that President James Buchanan had dispatched federal troops to quell a supposed "Mormon rebellion." He started for Utah immediately to inform Brigham Young. Hoping to reach a peaceful settlement before the army reached Utah, Brigham asked Daniel Wells, Porter Rockwell, Major Lot Smith, Ephraim Hanks, and a few other select men to slow down the army by harassing them and disrupting their supply wagons. Porter and the other men, who were nicknamed the Mormon Raiders, were successful in their efforts. This gave time for Colonel Thomas L. Kane, an influential friend of the Mormons, time to meet with the new governor, Alfred Cumming, and other dignitaries at Camp Scott.

When Thomas was able to persuade Governor Cumming and a few officials to go to Salt Lake City and meet with Church leaders, Porter met the men just outside the army's camp, explaining that Brigham had sent him to escort them safely to the valley.

As the group traveled down Echo Canyon, Governor Cumming and the other officials took note of the many campfires burning in the canyon. They were halted numerous times by small bands of Mormons who interrogated them before letting them pass. By the time Governor Cumming reached the mouth of the canyon, he estimated he had seen between two to three thousand Mormons.[32]

However, Cumming was the victim of an elaborate hoax. The militia had started phony, unmanned campfires. The men who had repeatedly stopped the governor's buggy were actually the same men—after interrogating the federal officials, they had ridden ahead in order to be at the next stop in the canyon. By the time Governor Cumming arrived in Salt Lake City, he was convinced that Johnston's Army didn't stand a chance of getting through the canyon with so many Mormons guarding it. Cumming decided it would be necessary to negotiate peace at any cost. Eventually, a peaceful settlement was reached and the Utah War ended.

In addition to his duties as a deputy marshal, Porter built a stage station near the Point of the Mountain to provide a rest stop for Overland Stage passengers. Porter took care of the stable and hired men to tend the hotel and bar.[33]

President Young occasionally visited Porter's station. Records indicate he stopped twice—in September 1862, and once in May 1863.[34]

Brigham and Porter remained close friends, as evidenced by the Brigham's appearance at a Church trial, which was convened when Porter accused Israel Evans of stealing an ox. Brigham Young rarely handled such matters, but he conducted this trial, which was held on 26 January 1861. As a result of this investigation, Evans was disfellowshipped.[35]

Because of Porter's unsurpassed tracking skills, people often asked him to track their stolen livestock. In July 1869, Porter helped a rancher named Nelson to track down ten of his best horses, which had been stolen by two thieves. The *Deseret News* publicly thanked Porter for his assistance in recovering the stolen horses.[36]

When Porter returned home from this assignment, he discovered that Brigham Young had been arrested for violating the recently passed anti-polygamy bill. When President Young appeared in court, Chief Justice Kinney demanded $2,000 in bail before Brigham could be released. Porter and three other men stepped forward to provide the money and sign bonds to have Brigham released.[37] Brigham was later acquitted by a grand jury.

Although rumors continued to circulate accusing Porter of various crimes, including murder, he was apparently in good enough standing to participate in Church and civic duties. The Deseret News reported that during a trial, a judge saw Porter in the audience and asked him to be sworn in for duty as a bailiff.[38]

Porter also found time to preach occasionally. On 28 January 1858, William Marsden, wrote in his journal, "Whent [sic] to Meeting at Night when Porter Rockwell preached."[39]

When Porter's wife, Mary Ann, died after giving birth in September of 1866, Porter closed down the station and moved it into the city. Approximately five years later, Porter married Christina Olsen.

Around this time, prosecutors began going after Church leaders who practiced plural marriage. Brigham was out in bail in 1872 for this charge when he left Salt Lake City to go to St. George, where he lived during the winter. After Brigham's departure, Judge McKean, one of Brigham's enemies, unexpectedly allowed the prosecutor to move up Brigham's trial to December.

It was generally felt at the time that Judge McKean and the prosecutor knew that traveling back to Salt Lake City over rough, pitted roads in the cold of winter would be hard on the aging Brigham. Yet if he did not return in time for the trial, Brigham would forfeit a $5,000 bond.

When lawyers could only postpone Brigham's trial until January 9, Porter saddled his fastest horse and rode south. He found Brigham in Cedar City on December 20. Knowing that Brigham suffered from rheumatism and would be in great pain during the long, rough trip back to Salt Lake City, Porter advised him not to return; however, Brigham insisted.

A heavy mackinaw, gloves, and a lap robe was no protection against a fierce winter storm. Although the jolting caused Brigham much pain, he was able to arrive in time for the trial. During the court session, it was obvious that Brigham was old and frail. Because of that, Judge McKean allowed Brigham to be held in custody at his home—under guard from a United States Marshal— instead of being sent to the penitentiary. Later, because of irregularities in Judge McKean's proceedings, the charges against Brigham were dropped and all pending indictments were dismissed.[40]

In June 1873, Brigham asked Porter Rockwell and George W. Bean to move to central Utah to start a new settlement, and to work with the Indians. They arrived with a group of settlers in August and after the colony was established, Porter returned home, where he pursued mining and ranching concerns, worked in law enforcement, and continued his missionary labors.

In September 1877, one month after the death of Brigham Young, Porter was arrested for the murder of John Aiken, who had been killed nineteen years before. Porter was released from jail when his friends posted bail, and a trial was set for October 1878. However, before he could come to trial, Porter died of heart failure on 9 June 1878.

Joseph F. Smith, a member of the Quorum of the Twelve Apostles, spoke at Porter's funeral, which was attended by nearly 1,000 people. He said, "He had his . . . faults, but Porter's life on earth, taken altogether, was one worthy of example . . . Through all of his trials he had never once forgotten his obligations to his brethren and his God."[41]

Nickolas Van Alfen gave the following tribute; "With his peculiar talents as a missionary, he [Porter] helped establish Zion in the tops of the mountains. He became a terror to the lawless elements of early Utah. He stood ready at the call of any friend to regain stolen cattle or horses. He rode thousands of miles in the severest weather in the service of the Church. Only Rockwell could have endured such hardships. . . . This Porter considered being true to the kingdom, for he did not accept any money for his services."[42]

Notes

1. Fitz Hugh Ludlow, *The Heart of the Continent: A Record of Travel Across the Plains and in Oregon, With an Examination of the Mormon Principle* (New York: 1870), 354–55.

2. George Washington Bean, *Autobiography of George Washington Bean, a Utah pioneer of 1847, and his family records*, Flora Diana Bean Horne, comp. (Salt Lake City: Utah Printing Co., 1945), 175–76.

3. Elizabeth D. E. Roundy, "Ancestry of Orrin Porter Rockwell" (printed without attribution), the *Deseret News*, Church Section, 31 Aug. 1935, 7.

4. Harold Schindler, *Orrin Porter Rockwell, Man of God, Son of Thunder* (Salt Lake City: University of Utah Press, 1966), 17.

5. Bean, *Autobiography of George Washington Bean, a Utah pioneer of 1847, and his family records*, Horne, comp., 175.

6. Richard Lloyd Dewey, *Porter Rockwell, A Biography* (New York: Paramount Books, 1986), 44.

7. John C. Bennet, *The History of the Saints: an Exposé of Joe Smith and Mormonism* (Boston: 1842), 283.

8. *History of the Church*, vol. 5 (Salt Lake City: The Church of Jesus Christ of Latter-day Saints, 1950), 125.

9. Roundy, "Ancestry of Orrin Porter Rockwell," 7.

10. *Journal History of the Church*, vol. VI, (Salt Lake City: The Church of Jesus Christ of Latter-day Saints, 1950), 134–35.

11. Mary Audentia Smith Anderson, ed., condensed by Bertha Audentia Anderson Hulmes, *Joseph Smith III and the Restoration* (Independence: Herald House, 1952), 76–77.

12. *Journal History of the Church of Jesus Christ of Latter-day Saints*, 14, 31 March; 2, 19 April; and 8 May 1846 (Salt Lake City: LDS Church History Library).

13. *Journal History of the Church of Jesus Christ of Latter-day Saints*, 25 August 1846 (Salt Lake City: LDS Church History Library).

14. Porter was made a Deputy Sheriff after Utah was organized as a Territory on 9 September 1850.

15. Nickolas Van Alfen, "Orrin Porter Rockwell," *Chronicles of Courage*, vol. 6 (Salt Lake City: International Society Daughters of Utah Pioneers, 1995), 390.

16. Roundy, "Ancestry of Orrin Porter Rockwell," 7.

17. Merrill D. Beal, *Henry Allen Beal and George Washington Bean, Pioneers on the Utah Frontier* (Garland: V. W. Johns Printing, 1971), 106.

18. *Journal History of the Church of Jesus Christ of Latter-day Saints*, 11 October 1847, (Salt Lake City: LDS Church History Library).

19. *Bean, Autobiography of George Washington Bean, a Utah pioneer of 1847, and his family records*, Horne, comp., 53–55.

20. Ibid., 175.

21. At this time, abstinence was not yet a Church commandment. Brigham would not issue it as such for several years.

22. *Journal History of the Church of Jesus Christ of Latter-day Saints*, 12 November 1850 (Salt Lake City: LDS Church History Library).

23. Israel Bennion, "Incidents relating to Orrin Porter Rockwell" (Unpublished document on file at Salt Lake City: LDS Church Archives), 3.

24. *Journal History of the Church of Jesus Christ of Latter-day Saints*, 3 June 1851 (Salt Lake City: LDS Church History Library).

25. Bean, *Autobiography of George Washington Bean, a Utah pioneer of 1847, and his family records*, Horne, comp., 95.

26. Conway B. Sonne, *World of Wakara* (San Antonio: The Naylor Company, 1962), 192–95.

27. Ibid., 202.

28. Dewey, *Porter Rockwell, A Biography*, 178.

29. Roundy, "Ancestry of Orrin Porter Rockwell," 7.

30. Jules Remy and Julius Brenchley, M.A., *A Journey to Great Salt Lake City*, vol. 2 (London: Printed by John Edward Taylor, 1861), 314–15.

31. *Deseret News Weekly*, 3 Jun. 1857, 101.

32. Hubert Howe Bancroft, *History of Utah* (Salt Lake City: Bookcraft, 1964), 526n.

33. Running a tavern while remaining in good standing in the Church appears a contradiction, but at this time, many members looked at abstinence as a minor rule, since until very recently, it had only been considered "by way of suggestion."

34. *Journal History of the Church of Jesus Christ of Latter-day Saints*, 4 September 1862; 25 September 1862; and 19 May 1863 (Salt Lake City: LDS Church History Library).

35. Schindler, *Orrin Porter Rockwell, Man of God, Son of Thunder*, 311.

36. Ibid., 353.

37. *Journal History of the Church of Jesus Christ of Latter-day Saints*, 9 March 1863 (Salt Lake City: LDS Church History Library).

38. *Journal History of the Church of Jesus Christ of Latter-day Saints*, 2 April 1863 (Salt Lake City: LDS Church History Library).

39. Dewey, *Porter Rockwell, A Biography*, 234.

40. Leonard J. Arrington, *Brigham Young, American Moses* (Urbana: University of Illinois Press, 1986), 373.

41. Schindler, *Orrin Porter Rockwell, Man of God, Son of Thunder*, 368.

42. Van Alfen, "Orrin Porter Rockwell," *Chronicles of Courage*, Vol. 6, 388.

Lot Smith

1830–1892

Lot Smith, an experienced frontiersman and military officer, was a man Brigham Young depended upon to help colonize new settlements, serve as a body guard, protect the telegraph line, guard those transporting the mail, and assist in military operations.

As a military officer, Lot earned the rank of major.

> Of all the officers of the early Utah Militia, Lot Smith stood at the top in his ability and wide experience in actual field service. A member of Company E of the Mormon Battalion . . . as a colleague of Robert T. Burton in the Fort Utah skirmish in 1849, as a member of General Wells' staff from 1849 onward, as a participant in the Walker Indian War in 1853, as one of the most active officers at the time of the Utah Expedition in 1857, he finally commanded the only Utah troops in the Civil War in 1862. Afterwards he rode south with militia companies in the Black Hawk Indian War between 1865 and 1867.[1]

Lot Smith was a large man, standing over six feet tall and weighing between 200 and 250 pounds. He had a reddish beard and steel-blue eyes. Lot was born 15 May 1830 in Williams, New York. After his conversion,

Lot moved to Nauvoo, then left with the Saints because of severe persecution. The Mormons were working their way west when the United States Government offered to let them provide a battalion of soldiers to march to California. Brigham Young encouraged the men to join, telling them that their pay would enable the Saints to buy supplies for their westward journey. Lot Smith immediately volunteered. "Lot served his country in the fear of God and with good will to man in the Mormon Battalion. He was, perhaps the youngest man that bore arms in that military body, being only sixteen years of age, but being large in stature he was accepted."[2]

One time Lot and the Mormon Battalion were crossing a desert when they ran out of water. Lot wrote:

> One day when we had marched a long distance without water, and nearly famished, we beheld a dry lake at a distance, sometimes called a mirage . . . and we traveled six miles across this delusion and still found no water, and night had fully come.
>
> When the men dug down about eight feet, they found abundance to supply all our wants . . . I was selected to go back with a keg of water on a mule to help those who had fallen by the way, who numbered quite a few. I had instructions not to give any one any water till I got back to the last man and then I was to work back to the company, having very particular instructions . . . I soon met a man who was anxiously enquiring for water . . . I put him off, also the second, third and fourth, I think, but from this on I could no longer stand their pleadings. I watered them all and had some left, so I had a drink when I got through a distance of twelve or fourteen miles . . . The Lord surely blessed my little keg of water in a marvelous manner. For my disobedience to orders I was tied behind a wagon and made to walk in trying circumstances which rather humiliated me, but I felt I could not have done less.[3]

After serving his time in the Mormon Battalion, Lot went to Utah and settled in Farmington, a small town north of Salt Lake City. While there, he was called to serve as President of one of the Quorums of the Seventy. Lot also acted as a special body guard to Brigham Young, accompanying the Prophet on all trips north and south of Salt Lake City. In 1854, Lot Smith was elected Sheriff of Davis and Morgan Counties—the first elected law man in Davis County, Utah. Lot served in this position until 1859.[4]

When his younger brother, Hyrum, was killed in an accident ten days before his scheduled marriage to Julia Ann Smith (no relation), Lot married Julia for time and she was sealed to Hyrum for eternity in the Endowment House on 25 November 1855. Lot's friend, Brigham Young, performed the ceremony.

In 1857, Brigham Young found out that a United States army of 2,500 infantry, artillery, and dragoons was on its way to Utah under General Johnston to put down an alleged Mormon "insurrection" and to install a new governor. Since Brigham had not been formally notified by the government of this action, he regarded the soldiers as invaders and called upon his influential friend Colonel Thomas L. Kane to act as a mediator between the Mormons and the United States Government.

Since the army was already on their way to Utah, Brigham knew he had to slow them down in order to allow time for Colonel Kane to reach the army and negotiate a peaceful settlement with the federal officials that were traveling with the soldiers.

To delay the army, President Young turned to a number of frontiersmen, including Major Lot Smith, to do everything they could to slow the army. They blocked mountain passes, stampeded the army's animals, set fire to captured supply wagons, and burned forage for the army's livestock.

Lot felt it was his sacred duty to protect the Saints from the invading army and worked diligently to fulfill his assignment. C. L. Christensen, one of Lot's closest friends, said, "There never was a man that held the life and liberty of man more sacred than did Lot Smith."[5] Christensen went on to say, "During the Echo Canyon war [often referred to as the Utah War] he [Lot] played a brave and noble part and did it well under the circumstances. He had instructions from President Brigham Young to 'shed no blood,' and not even to fire a gun unless absolutely in self-defense. Lot was so prompt in carrying out this advice that several men in his charge left him and went home, they having a desire of gaining fame otherwise than according to the advice that Lot held and kept most sacred."[6]

Lot Smith, Porter Rockwell, Ephraim Hanks, and the other men who were assigned to slow down the army were called the "Mormon Raiders." One federal soldier, Henry Hamilton, recalled how these men harassed them, saying, "The Mormons now began to trouble us considerably, impeding our progress in various ways, and making it as difficult for us as possible. Every day when coming to camp they [the Mormons] would set the grass on fire, using long torches, and riding swift horses, so that before pitching tents we always had to fight fire. They destroyed so much of it that the animals had to be driven some distance to get feed."[7]

At first, the harassment had little effect in slowing the army. Then, during one very successful raid, the Mormon Raiders were able to capture seventy-four supply wagon trains. This significantly slowed the army's advance because they could not continue on until new supplies arrived. The supplies the wagons carried—vegetables, bread, coffee, flour, bacon, vinegar, and soap—would have lasted the army three months.[8]

Then, on October 4, Major Lot Smith and his riders captured two more wagon trains. Lot told the captain of the train, Mr. Dawson, to get all of his men and their private property out of the wagons and to disengage the animals because he was going to burn the wagons.

Mr. Dawson exclaimed, "For God's sake, don't burn the [wagon] trains!"

Lot replied that "it [is] for His sake that [I am] going to burn them."[9]

Around this time, Captain Van Vliet of the United States Army went to Salt Lake City to see Brigham Young and other Church leaders to discuss the situation. Captain Van Vliet said that General Johnston insisted that his army be allowed to march through Salt Lake City. Brigham Young was vehemently opposed to this. He informed Captain Van Vliet that he had evacuated most of the Saints, but had ordered a few men to stay in various spots around the city. The new governor and other federal officials were welcome to come, Brigham said, but if the army entered Salt Lake City, he would order the men he had placed at strategic locations to set fire to houses, barns, stores and all other buildings, as well as trees and vegetation. The men were waiting for his signal, Brigham said, even now, and had torches ready to be lit at a moment's notice. In addition, Brigham flatly refused to sell any provisions to the army, which he still regarded as an invading force.

Later, Brigham spoke to the Saints about the success the Mormon Raiders were having in slowing down the army: "We have already showed the invading army a few tricks; and I told Captain Van Vliet that if they persisted in making war upon us, I should share in their supplies. The boys would ride among the enemy's tents . . . if you don't look out."[10]

Brigham's boast came true. One federal soldier reported: "One morning, just before daybreak, they [Mormon Raiders] rushed through the camp, firing guns and yelling like Indians, driving off all our mules and horses, numbering about a thousand, and before we could get into line they were safely out of reach of our rifles. It was ten o'clock before we recovered our animals. They hovered around daily, watching and taking every advantage of us, feeling safe in their tactics, knowing our inability to cope with them, as we had no cavalry, while they had the fleetest of horses.[11]

Major Lot Smith and other Mormon Raiders were able to destroy many supply wagons and capture fourteen hundred of the army's two thousand cattle. Because of this, the army was forced to winter over in Fort Bridger, which the Mormons had burned on the inside so that the army could not use it against them.[12] All the cattle that were captured were herded to Salt Lake City, taken care of, and returned to the army the following summer.[13]

After Thomas L. Kane reached Johnston's army at Camp Scott, he was able to convince the new governor, Alfred Cumming, and some federal officials to go with him to Salt Lake City. After meeting Brigham Young, Governor Cumming asked about the court records that, according to the testimony of previous justices, Brigham had burned. President Young led him to a clerk's office and showed him the documents.

When Governor Cumming asked why the city appeared so deserted, Brigham explained that he wanted the people out of danger should the army march against the city and had told the people to go south to Provo. He said that unless a peaceful solution could be reached, the Saints would continue on south, perhaps going as far as Mexico.

During the negotiations, Governor Cumming went to Provo himself and asked the people to return, but they would not. Finally, at the end of June, a compromise was reached. Brigham agreed to let the troops march through Salt Lake City on three conditions: 1) the soldiers must be unarmed; 2) they must not stop in the city, but continue marching until they reached the Jordan River, a few miles west of the city; 3) after a rest, the army was to march south another thirty-six miles before making camp. Once the army was safely ensconced at Camp Floyd in Cedar Valley, Brigham told the Saints it was safe to return to their homes.

President Buchanan's hasty action in ordering United States troops to Utah without taking time to investigate the justices' reports, which were later found to be full of falsehoods, became known as "Buchanan's Blunder." In an attempt to offset the embarrassment this incident caused, President Buchanan publicly offered Brigham Young a full pardon for his supposed treason and other crimes, including those committed by the Mormon Raiders as they tried to slow down the advancing army.

When President Young received President Buchanan's "pardon," he replied, "As far as I am concerned, I thank President Buchanan for forgiving me, but I really cannot tell what I have done. I know one thing, and that is that the people called Mormons are a loyal and law-abiding people, and have ever been. . . . It is true Lot Smith burned some wagons containing government supplies for the army. This was an overt act, and if it is for this we are to be pardoned, I accept the pardon."[14]

On 3 January 1858, Lot married Laura Lousia Burdick, the first wife to whom he was sealed for time and all eternity. In later years, he married other wives. Three years later, Lot was elected to the State Legislature.

In 1861, the acting governor, Frank Fuller, asked Brigham Young if the Mormons could supply a force of twenty mounted men for thirty days to protect mail and telegraph lines on the Overland Trail, which went from Fort Bridger to the Sierra Nevada Mountains. Brigham agreed, asking Major Lot Smith to direct a group of volunteers, who were shortly on their way. After reaching Independence Rock, the Mormon troops joined with Colonel William O. Collins, who was the acting divisional commander. Many found it ironic that Lot Smith and his men, the nemesis of Johnston's Army, were now officially part of the United States Army and were assigned duty alongside government troops near the North Platte River.

A year later, in 1862, Abraham Lincoln called upon Brigham Young for help. Lincoln had rerouted the transcontinental stage lines through Salt Lake City in an attempt to put them out of the reach of confederate troops. However, because it was difficult to differentiate between friend and foe, the new route required military protection. In addition, those transporting the mail had to be protected, since mail drivers were frequently attacked and killed, with outlaws, Indians, and confederate sympathizers destroying the mail. Marauders also frequently destroyed newly-completed telegraph lines.

Because of the Civil War, President Lincoln could not spare any troops to protect stage lines, mail drivers, or telegraph lines. Abraham Lincoln was well aware of Brigham's influence in Utah and contacted him instead of Utah's acting governor, Frank Fuller, to "Raise, arm and equip a company of Calvary for ninety days service, to protect the property of the telegraph and overland mail companies."[15]

Brigham Young chose one of his most trusted men, Lot Smith, to fill this assignment. Lot and his group of one hundred and six men left on 14 August 1862 to protect the overland mail route.[16] It is possible that part of the reason Lincoln called upon Brigham Young was because one of the mail companies was run by the Mormons. Another reason might have been because Brigham had already told government officials that "the Militia of Utah [the Nauvoo Legion] are ready and able and willing to protect the mail line if called upon to do so."[17]

Sometime between 1864 and 1865, Lot Smith saw a beautiful, unbroken horse that belonged to Brigham Young. The horse had Arabian blood and was quite valuable, but when Lot admired the animal, people warned him to stay away, saying the horse was vicious.

When Lot found out it was one of six matched horses, he offered to break the animal for Brigham, but President Young said, "No Lot, I think too much of you to risk your life in that manner." However, when Lot persisted, Brigham sent him the horse.

When Lot came back with the horse, which he had named Stonewall, he was riding the animal. After Lot dismounted, he took hold of the horse by the hind legs, raising them up and down to demonstrate how docile the horse was. He then left. To everyone's surprise, Stonewall followed Lot home. When Lot returned the horse, President Young said, "Lot, because you broke that horse in such a wonderful manner, I will make you a present of him."[18]

In July 1869, Lot went on a two-year mission to Great Britain. After his return, he was elected to the Legislative Assembly for the Territories of Davis and Morgan Counties in August 1871.

One of the last colonies Brigham Young started was on the Little Colorado River. Although initial reports about the area were not positive, Brigham felt that colonizing that section of Arizona was important. In mid-January 1876, Brigham appointed Lot Smith and James Brown as leaders over the Little Colorado expedition. Along with over two hundred men, women, and children, Lot and James traveled six hundred miles to this new area. Their assignment was to establish settlements in the Arizona Territory and to work among the Indians, introducing them to the gospel.[19] Because his company had to leave before melting snow made fording the rivers impossible, Lot was only given ten days to get ready so they could leave on 3 February 1876.

The Arizona colony became a success—due largely to Lot Smith's skill and experience as a frontiersman and his promptness in heeding Brigham Young's counsel. One of Lot's close friends, C. L. Christensen, wrote, "And many were the good and instructive letters he received from President Young in that early day which he would read in public and always advise the people to carry them out punctually."[20]

Lot had always agreed with Brigham's policy of feeding, not fighting the Indians and a good part of Lot's success as a colonizer was a result of his ability to get along so well with the Indians. "He visited the different tribes often and always enquired of their welfare and asked if any of our people were intruding on their rights, often enquiring if we were welcome in their land. . . . He was kind to them, feeding them and aiding them otherwise and he stood high with the Navajo chiefs."[21]

Brigham Young always liked to give detailed instructions to new settlers and in March of 1877, wrote Lot and other company captains in the Arizona mission. Brigham advised the leaders to place their settlements five miles apart but no more than twenty-five, to have fifty men in each settlement, to build on solid ground, erect corrals quickly, and to distribute the mechanics (skilled artisans) equally among the companies. In just one month, four settlements had been founded; Sunset, Brigham City, Obid, and St. Joseph. The settlers busily put in crops, planted gardens, and built houses.[22]

Although Brigham Young died in August 1877, Lot stayed on his mission. In 1878, he became President of the Little Colorado Stake of Zion. When Wilford Woodruff decided to see the Saints in Arizona, Lot accompanied him as he visited the various settlements, reorganizing nearly all of the stakes in Arizona. Wilford wrote, "On Sunday the 18 April 1979 I met with the Saints of both settlements in the dining hall . . . I stopped with Brother Lot Smith who is president of the stake. I took my meals with him at a family table."[23]

Lot Smith died in Arizona on 21 June 1892, after being shot by a renegade Indian. At his funeral, the following was reported: "John Sharp said, 'There lies a man who never knew fear. He was as gentle as a woman and brave as a lion. I knew him as a citizen, as a soldier, and also as a missionary of the church, when he was a humble preacher in a foreign land. He was always the same brave, true, genial, kind hearted man. His soul was full of good cheer and love.' There were many other speakers and the last [was] President Joseph F. Smith [who] called Lot a generous, noble hearted man. He was such that history will record the fact that Lot Smith was one of the notable figures of the past. In every instance he discharged his duty to the best of his ability."[24]

Notes

1. Hamilton Gardner, *Pioneer Military Leaders of Utah*, (Unpublished document on file at Salt Lake City: LDS Church History Library, 1952), 58.

2. Andrew Jenson, *Latter-day Saint Biographical Encyclopedia*, vol. 1 (Andrew Jenson History Company: Salt Lake City), 803–4.

3. Ibid., 804.

4. Nona Smith Rhead, *Lot Smith: Captain, Colonizer, Churchman, 1830–1892* (Unpublished manuscript on file at Salt Lake City: LDS Church History Library), 3.

5. Jenson, *Latter-day Saint Biographical Encyclopedia*, vol. 1, 803.

6. Ibid., 803–4.

7. Henry S. Hamilton, *Reminiscences of a Veteran* (Concord: Republican Press Association, 1897), 80.

8. Leonard J. Arrington, *Great Basin Kingdom, An Economic History of the Latter-day Saints 1830–1900* (Cambridge: Harvard University Press, 1958), 178.

9. Lot Smith "The Echo Canyon War," *The Contributor*, vol. 3 (1882), 273.

10. *Journal of Discourses*, 26 volumes (London: Latter-day Saints' Book Depot, 1854–86), 176.

11. Hamilton, *Reminiscences of a Veteran*, 80–81.

12. Arnold K. Garr, Donald Q. Cannon, Richard O. Cowan, eds. *Encyclopedia of Latter-day Saint History* (Salt Lake City; Deseret Book, 2000), 1283.

13. Arrington, *Great Basin Kingdom, An Economic History of the Latter-day Saints 1830–1900*, 178.

14. Clarissa Young Spencer and Mabel Harmer, *Brigham Young at Home* (Salt Lake City: Deseret Book Company, 1940), 106.

15. Francis M. Gibbons, *Brigham Young, Modern Moses/Prophet of God* (Salt Lake City: Deseret Book, 1981), 221.

16. "Departure of the Company for the Protection of the Mail and Telegraph Lines," *Deseret News*, 7 May 1862, 357.

17. Gustive O. Larson, "Utah and the Civil War," *Utah Historical Quarterly*, 33 (Winter 1965), 59.

18. Rhead, *Lot Smith: Captain, Colonizer, Churchman, 1830–1892*, 6.

19. H. Dean Garrett, "The Honeymoon Trail," *Ensign*, Jul. 1989, 24.

20. Jenson, *Latter-day Saint Biographical Encyclopedia*, vol. 1, 805.

21. C.L. Christensen, as quoted by Jenson, *Latter-day Saint Biographical Encyclopedia*, vol. 1, 803–804.

22. Leonard J. Arrington, *Brigham Young, American Moses* (Urbana: University of Illinois Press, 1986), 383.

23. Rhead, *Lot Smith: Captain, Colonizer, Churchman, 1830–1892*, 11.

24. Ibid., 21.

Hosea Stout

1810–1889

Hosea Stout was a skilled outdoorsman who was deeply loyal to Joseph Smith and Brigham Young. Early historian Andrew Jenson said of Hosea: "In his youth he was very intimate with the Prophet Joseph Smith and served as one of the Prophet's bodyguards. Afterwards he became a true and staunch friend of President Brigham Young, who placed the utmost confidence in his ability and integrity."[1]

At Nauvoo, Hosea served as the Captain of Police. He was also a commander in the Nauvoo Legion. Brigham authorized Hosea to serve in similar capacities at Winter Quarters and during the trek west.

Hosea Stout kept a comprehensive journal that gives much insight into Brigham Young. Although Brigham was demanding at times, he had many outstanding leadership traits, such as fearlessness, tenacity, wisdom, mercy, and a complete fidelity to the people he served.

Hosea Stout was born 18 September 1810, at Danville, Kentucky. When he was eighteen, Hosea moved to Illinois and taught school before moving to Missouri in 1837. He married Samantha Peck on 7 January 1838 and was baptized later that year.

The Saints were facing severe persecution at this time, and in October 1838, a company of Missouri militia captured three Mormons. When the Missourians threatened to kill the men, Church leaders asked for volunteers to go rescue the prisoners. Hosea was among those who participated in what became known as the Battle of Crooked River. David W. Patten was shot during the conflict and Hosea was the first to reach the mortally wounded Apostle who died later that night from his injuries. Not long after, Hosea and twenty-five other men were forced to flee for their lives.

The Saints were subsequently expelled from Missouri, and Hosea went to Quincy, then to Nauvoo, where he was appointed as a clerk for the High Council. His wife, Samantha, passed away while at Nauvoo, and in 1840, Hosea married Louisa Taylor. He later practiced polygamy.

When the Nauvoo Legion was organized, Hosea served as a second lieutenant. He soon became a captain and then a colonel. For a time, Hosea even served as acting brigadier-general. As an active and efficient officer, Hosea Stout valiantly defended Nauvoo from mobs. He also served on the Nauvoo police force and was eventually appointed Chief of Police.

When a mob of Missourians tried to kidnap Joseph Smith in 1841, Hosea risked his life by putting himself in the front ranks during a rescue attempt. Hosea was elected a trustee of a mercantile and mechanical association, and worked on the Nauvoo temple.

Early in 1844, when the Prophet Joseph called for volunteers to go to the Rocky Mountains to seek out a new home for the Saints, Hosea Stout was among the first to respond. However, because of Joseph Smith's death, that expedition never went. That April, Hosea went on a short mission to Kentucky.

During the general exodus from Nauvoo in 1846, Brigham asked Hosea to oversee a police force of about one hundred men, whose assignment was to assist and protect the Saints. Gathering a collection of old flatboats and skiffs, Hosea superintended the movement of the Saints across the Mississippi River. As the weather grew colder and the river froze, some of the wagons were able to cross on the ice.

The first general encampment was made at Sugar Creek, which was close enough to Nauvoo that Brigham could direct the evacuation of the rest of the Saints. The first thing Brigham did after arriving at Sugar Creek was to appoint Hosea as Captain of the Guard.[2]

Hosea kept a detailed journal and recorded many incidents that show Brigham Young's able leadership. While Hosea sometimes complained about Brigham's habit of changing orders and plans, he seemed to understand that this came from a need to adjust to developing problems.

By March 1846, the Saints were ready to leave Sugar Creek, a temporary base from which Brigham planned to have the Saints leapfrog to other encampments spread out across Iowa. Brigham directed men to go ahead and build bridges, and prepare the road for the Saints. As teams and wagons began leaving Sugar Creek, Hosea Stout and his men stood guard and protected the caravans.

Hosea, like many of the Saints, suffered from lack of food. Once, Hosea said that Brigham "inquired into and I related to him my situation and the suffering that I had passed through. . . . He borrowed 109 pounds of flour for me . . . and said I could borrow any thing that I needed [and] he would see it paid. . . . My prospects for living seemed to brighten for he acted like a friend that was willing to help in time of need."[3]

Brigham Young worked continually to improve the organization of the companies and to establish colonies at Garden Grove and Mount Pisgah. He directed the first companies to plant crops, which would be harvested later by following groups. Hosea moved with the Saints along the trail, helping those in need. After arriving at Council Bluffs on June 14, Hosea established a ferry and worked with the Indian agency and the Omaha Indians for permission for the Saints to settle temporarily on their land.

In June, the Saints learned that the United States had offered to let the Mormons organize a battalion of five hundred soldiers to march to Santa Fe against Mexico and from there, to go to California. Hosea, like many of the Saints, was deeply distrustful of this idea. He said, "We were very indignant at this requisition and only looked on it as a plot laid to bring trouble on us as a people."[4]

Brigham Young, who had sent Jesse C. Little to petition the government for some form of aid for the Saints, was initially leery of this proposal. However, after discussing it with Jesse and others, Brigham realized that the offer was a friendly gesture—one that would provide great benefits to the Saints. The cash paid to the soldiers would buy supplies to finance the Saints' westward migration, while the entire Battalion would be transported west wholly at the government's expense. In addition, providing an enlistment of Mormon men would do much to dispel the charge of many politicians in Washington who were claiming that the Mormons were disloyal to the United States. Seeing this opportunity as a blessing, Brigham Young asked the Saints to go along with the government's proposal.

Hosea still had some questions about the battalion, so he asked to talk with President Young privately. Later, he wrote, "I had a few minutes interview with President Young who briefly told me that they were going to comply with the requisitions of the President . . . and that there was a good feeling existing between us and him and all was right."[5]

On 26 September 1846, Hosea was appointed lieutenant-colonel in the Nauvoo Legion. When the headquarters of the Church moved to Winter Quarters that same month, Brigham appointed Hosea as Chief of Police.

Camp life was difficult and Hosea worried that the ongoing pressure of moving the Saints might wear Brigham down. Wanting to lighten Brigham's heavy load of responsibility, Hosea reprimanded his men severely on 15 March 1846, for "continually running to [President Brigham] Young for advice and council about matters which had already been laid down."[6]

With winter fast approaching, and over ten thousand Saints still camped between Nauvoo and Grand Island, Brigham turned his attention to building homes and settling the people for the winter. While overseeing the Saint's physical welfare, Brigham remained concerned about their spirituality. One of his fears was that going into the wilderness might cause some of the Saints to transgress freely, thinking that they would not be held accountable. Brigham said, "I was not so much afraid of going into the wilderness alone, as to let offenders go unpunished."[7]

To stave off this problem, Brigham Young gave precise instructions regarding countless issues—from drunkenness to improperly tying up dogs. To maintain peace and stability among the Saints, Brigham saw to it that Hosea Stout, as head of the police, disciplined those who transgressed. On September 4, Hosea directed that some unchaste young men be whipped, commenting that this was "the first step taken since we were in the wilderness to enforce obedience to the Law of God."[8]

On 14 January 1847, Brigham Young received a revelation detailing how the Saints should be organized for the trip to the Rocky Mountains and how to take care of the needy. Hosea records, "Here the subject of our removal in the Spring was taken up and the order adopted how we should go and sustain the poor in the mein time."[9]

Brigham and the Apostles then began visiting the various communities to present the revelation and begin the organizational process. Hosea met frequently with President Brigham Young and other Church leaders to make final plans for the westward trek. Early in 1847, Brigham asked

Hosea to go with him on the first trip and to be captain of the guard, but shortly after, he changed his mind, deciding Hosea's services were needed more at Winter Quarters.

Like most of the Saints, Hosea faced many trials and sorrow. After being expelled from Nauvoo and before leaving for the Salt Lake Valley, Hosea lost five members of his immediate family. Hosea was at Garden Grove when two of his sons died in his arms. One of them died of "whooping cough and black canker" on May 8. There is no record at to the cause of death for the second child. Then, at Winter Quarters, Hosea lost a newborn infant and his wife Marinda, who died during childbirth. Later, one of Hosea's sons died near Council Bluffs.[10]

After taking the first group of pioneers to the Salt Lake Valley, Brigham Young stayed only one month, long enough to galvanize the Saints into action and to recover from an illness that had struck shortly before arriving in the valley. While traveling back to Winter Quarters, Brigham stopped and talked to companies headed to the Rocky Mountains, giving them directions and advice.

A special camaraderie existed between Brigham Young and the men who worked with him in so complicated and important a task as relocating the Saints to the distant Salt Lake Valley. In the fall of 1847, Hosea Stout and a few other men rode west for two weeks just to meet Brigham Young and ride with him as he returned to Winter Quarters.

After meeting Brigham on 18 October 1847, Hosea said, "The whole of us was in a perfect extacy [sic] of joy and gladness." Even the formidable Brigham Young became emotional and told Hosea and his companions how grateful he was that they had come to meet him and how happy he was to see them. Hosea wrote, "The President said it was more joy, more satisfaction to meet us than a company of angels."[11]

In January 1848, Hosea Stout, along with others, signed a petition asking the federal government to establish a post office at Kanesville. That spring, after helping organize more companies for the westward trek, Hosea crossed the plains in Heber C. Kimball's company, arriving in Utah in September 1848.

Hosea Stout was an important political figure in early Utah. When the provisional government of the Territory of Deseret was organized on 26 May 1849, Hosea Stout was elected a member of the first legislative assembly. The following February, Hosea was chosen as the first Attorney General of the Utah Territory. In 1851, he became one of the first attorneys admitted to the bar in the Utah Territory.[12]

When the Nauvoo Legion was reorganized in Utah, Hosea was appointed first lieutenant. He also served on various committees that planned public celebrations for Independence Day, Pioneer Day, and other holidays.

At General Conference in October 1852, Brigham Young called Hosea on a mission to China. Before leaving, he was asked to supervise the large company of missionaries during their journey to different parts of the world. Hosea arrived in Hong Kong, China, on 27 April 1853, along with Elders Chapman, Duncan, Lewis, and Thompson. Unfortunately, the people were not willing to listen to the gospel message and two months later, the missionaries boarded a ship to come back to Utah.

Hosea returned to a tragic situation. After arriving at his home, he discovered that his wife Louisa, and his infant son had both died on the very day he had left for China. Hosea's children were gone, his brother had moved, and his house was occupied by strangers who knew nothing about the whereabouts of his family.

Hosea wrote:

> Here, not 14 months since was concentrated all my earthly happiness. Here, the confiding Louisa, the dearest object of my heart . . . how often I have rejoiced that I was blessed with that true, faithful and confiding wife. Here, then, was my ocean of affection and love. I left them by the command of the Lord to preach the gospel in foreign lands, and returned but not to them. Louisa was no more, the source of my happiness was beneath the cold sod while the very geniuse [sic] of desolation and loneliness seemed to brook over the scenes of by gone happiness. What did I find? Even my brother had removed into the country . . . A family of English saints, total stranger to me resided here and could give no account of neither family or friends.[13]

Eventually Hosea was able to locate his children and his brother.

In 1854, Hosea was elected a member of the House of Representatives and served on the committee for judiciary matters. In December 1856, Hosea became Speaker of the House, chairman of the code commissioners, a state prosecutor, and a United States Attorney. Hosea soon gained a reputation as a celebrated prosecuting attorney in the Third District court.

When the handcart pioneers became stranded by early snowstorms in the fall of 1856, Hosea answered Brigham Young's call and went to their rescue. In January 1857, Hosea was elected a regent of the Deseret University, and in April, was appointed judge advocate by the legislative assembly.

When Brigham discovered that Johnston's Army was marching to Utah, he called upon Hosea because of his extensive police and military experience. Always ready to defend his people, Hosea served in the Nauvoo Legion under the leadership of Daniel Wells, helping prepare defenses in Echo Canyon. He also served as a special messenger between the companies stationed in Echo Canyon and militia headquarters in Salt Lake City.

In 1861, Brigham called Hosea to go on a colonization mission to southern Utah to help build up the Cotton Mission. Hosea soon became a prominent leader in St. George. During his five years there, Hosea was commissioned as a district attorney and was made President of the High Council of the Southern Mission.[14]

When Hosea returned to Salt Lake City in 1866, he resumed his place in the legal profession. In 1870, Hosea was ordained a High Priest and asked to be an alternate member of the High Council of the Salt Lake Stake.

Around this time, Hosea had problems with a well-known leader in the Church. He was unable to resolve the matter and it was finally presented before the High Council. After deliberating on the situation, the council decided against Hosea. A few days later, Brigham Young talked to Hosea about this and in the brusque manner he sometimes used, remarked crustily, "I suppose now you will go and apostatize."

"Oh no," answered Bro. Stout. "The Church of Christ is as much my Church as it is theirs, and what you or any one else may do cannot affect my Church."[15]

In 1871, Hosea was arrested on a false charge of killing Richard Yates during the Utah War. After being confined for six months at Camp Douglas, Hosea was acquitted and released.

When Congress passed an anti-polygamy bill, prosecutors began tracking down and arresting Church leaders. Brigham Young had been charged with violating this law but was free on bail in 1872, when he went to St. George for the winter. He went to southern Utah every year because the warmer weather assuaged his rheumatism pains. When a prosecutor asked Judge McKean, whose aversion to President Young was well-known, to move up the date for Brigham's trial, McKean allowed the motion, knowing that Brigham had already gone south for the winter.

Porter Rockwell rode to alert Brigham of this new development, which forced the elderly Prophet to travel hurriedly back to Salt Lake City. The cold and snow made the journey an arduous one and the badly pitted roads caused President Young great pain. Hosea Stout met Brigham Young in Draper so he could brief the president on the judicial proceedings. During the ride to Salt Lake City on the Utah Southern Railroad, Hosea helped prepare Brigham to appear in court.[16]

Because of ill health, Hosea Stout retired from public life in 1877, the same year Brigham Young died. Hosea passed away 2 March 1889, at his home in Salt Lake City.

As a hard-working and well-respected attorney, Hosea had been active most of his life in city and state government. As one of the first lawyers appointed to the Territory, Hosea gained considerable fame as a state prosecutor and as an attorney for the United States government. Andrew Jenson, said of him, "Bro. Stout was noted for his fidelity to President Brigham Young, who, especially in matters connected with legal affairs, frequently consulted him. His judgment could always be relied upon as being on the side of right and equity."[17]

On 9 March 1889, the *Deseret News* printed a tribute to Hosea, saying in part: "He shared in the vicissitudes through which the Church passed. He served in the Black Hawk War, taught school in Illinois, was intimately associated with the Prophet Joseph Smith prior to his death, and for some time acted as his body guard. He was an officer of the Nauvoo Legion and Chief of Police. . . . He was a man of sterling integrity and excellent ability."[18]

Notes

1. Andrew Jenson, *Latter-day Saint Biographical Encyclopedia*, vol. 3 (Salt Lake City: Andrew Jenson History Company, 1914), 534.

2. Wayne Stout, *Hosea Stout: Utah's Pioneer Statesman* (Salt Lake City: Wayne Stout, 1953), 64.

3. Juanita Brooks, ed., *On The Mormon Frontier: The Diary of Hosea Stout, 1844–1861*, vol. 1 (Salt Lake City: University of Utah Press, 1964), 178–179.

4. Ibid., 172.

5. Juanita Brooks, ed., *On The Mormon Frontier, The Diary of Hosea Stout 1844–1861*, vol. 2 (Salt Lake City: University of Utah Press, 1964), 174.

6. Brooks, ed., *On The Mormon Frontier: The Diary of Hosea Stout, 1844–1861*, vol. 1, 138.

7. Eugene England, *Brother Brigham* (Salt Lake City: Bookcraft, Inc., 1980), 130.

8. Ibid.

9. Brooks, ed., *On The Mormon Frontier: The Diary of Hosea Stout, 1844–1861*, vol. 1, 227.

10. England, *Brother Brigham*, 112.

11. Brooks, ed., *On The Mormon Frontier: The Diary of Hosea Stout, 1844–1861*, vol. 1, 283.

12. Stout, *Hosea Stout: Utah's Pioneer Statesman*, 138.

13. Juanita Brooks, *On the Mormon Frontier: The Diary of Hosea Stout*, vol. 2, 456, 498.

14. James Godson Bleak, *Annals of the Southern Utah Mission* [1896] (Salt Lake City: LDS Church Archives), 157, 187.

15. Jenson, *Latter-day Saint Biographical Encyclopedia*, vol. 3, 533.

16. Leonard J. Arrington, *Brigham Young, American Moses* (Urbana: University of Illinois Press, 1986), 373.

17. Jenson, *Latter-day Saint Biographical Encyclopedia*, vol. 3, 533–534.

18. Stout, *Hosea Stout: Utah's Pioneer Statesman*, 252.

About the Author

Marlene Bateman Sullivan was born in Salt Lake City, Utah, and grew up in Sandy, Utah. She graduated from the University of Utah with a Bachelor of Arts degree in English. In June of 1974, she married Kelly R. Sullivan. They are the parents of seven children and have twelve grandchildren. Her hobbies are gardening, card-making, and reading. She and her husband reside in North Salt Lake, Utah.

Marlene has been published extensively in magazines and newspapers. Her first book, *Latter-day Saint Heroes and Heroines*, is a collection of true stories about people who risked their lives to defend the gospel. The sequel, *Latter-day Saint Heroes and Heroines*, Vol. 2, contains more stories of saints who faced extreme trials with faith and courage. Marlene's third book, *And There Were Angels Among Them*, consists of documented accounts of angelic visits in early LDS Church history. *Visits from Beyond the Veil* is another unique collection of authenticated angelic experiences. *By the Ministering of Angels* is Marlene's fifth book and relates stories of angels helping people through their earthly trials.